EXPLODING THE

Official Myths

+ + + + + + + + + + + + **OF THE** + + + + + + + + + + + +

LINCOLN
ASSASSINATION

JAMES
PERLOFF

BURLINGTON, MASSACHUSETTS

Also by James Perloff:

The Shadows of Power: The Council on Foreign Relations and the American Decline (1988)

Tornado in a Junkyard: The Relentless Myth of Darwinism (1999)

The Case against Darwin: Why the Evidence Should Be Examined (2002)

Freedom Shall Return (2003) (music CD)

Truth Is a Lonely Warrior: Unmasking the Forces behind Global Destruction (2013)

Thirteen Pieces of the Jigsaw: Solving Political, Cultural and Spiritual Riddles, Past and Present (2019)

COVID-19 and the Agendas to Come, Red-Pilled (2020)

Missing Saints, Missing Miracles (2022)

———————————

Published by Refuge Books, 25 South Bedford Street, Burlington MA 01803
www.jamesperloff.net

ISBN 13: 978-0-9668160-6-8
ISBN 10: 0-9668160-6-4

Library of Congress Control Number: 2024910063

Contents

Introduction   1

1. The Mainstream Narrative   5

2. Early Anomalies in the Assassination Story   11

3. Alleged Botched Assassinations   29

4. Stanton's Behavior Immediately Following the Assassination   35

5. In Pursuit of John Wilkes Booth   41

6. Was Booth the Man in the Barn?   51

7. The Law Gets Perverted   59

8. With Justice for None   75

9. Edwin M. Stanton and the Nature of Evidence   97

10. Booth and a Wider Conspiracy   109

Epilogue   145

Index   149

Introduction

Much has been said in alternative media about the Kennedy assassination in recent years, but the Lincoln assassination seems to have gradually faded to lower rungs of historical interest.

Back in the mid-1990s, I was waiting to meet someone in Belmont, Mass. Having some time to kill, I strolled over to the Belmont Public Library and browsed its history section. A book caught my attention: *Why Was Lincoln Murdered?* published in 1937 by Otto Eisenschiml. It looked quite interesting and I checked it out of the library.

At that particular time, I was exploring Civil War history. The Internet was not in wide use yet, but I read a volume of Abraham Lincon's letters and speeches, Jefferson Davis's *Rise and Fall of the Confederate Government*, and quite a few memoirs and diaries written by those who'd experienced the War Between the States.

I thought Eisenschiml's book the best analysis I'd ever seen of the Lincoln assassination. Not only did he do extensive primary research in government archives, and read countless books pertaining to the assassination—especially memoirs and other writings by direct witnesses to the murder, trial, and other associated activities—but he proved to be a first-class critical thinker, asking many logical questions that challenged the assassination's mainstream account. Cherry-picking evidence is easy to do to support a particular theory. Eisenschiml didn't do that; he considered all sides of a question and avoided broad speculation. He followed up with another outstanding book, *In the Shadow of Lincoln's Death* (1940).

My research into the Civil War culminated with my publishing an article about it in *Southern Partisan* magazine in 1997, after which I moved on to other things. That article didn't address the Lincoln assassination, but Eisenschiml's piercing insights have always stayed with me, and I feel the time has come to bring them to this generation.

Before beginning this book, I looked to see if any modern author had accomplished work comparable to Eisenschiml, and I found one in Don Thomas, who has done monumental research, accessing files that had been unavailable to Eisenschiml. He has written *The Reason Lincoln Had to Die* (2013) and *The Reason Booth Had to Die* (2017). His website is www.reasonlincoln.com.

I noticed that Don Thomas never referenced Eisenschiml, so when I first chatted with him, I asked if he didn't like something about Eisenschiml. It turned out that Thomas hadn't read the former's 87-year-old book, yet extensive research and sound logic had led both men independently to much the same conclusions.

I am indebted to Don for his analysis of the FBI's forensic exam of John Wilkes Booth's diary, his calling attention to the George Atzerodt confession found in 1977, his citing the significance of James Donaldson, Booth's whistle, and the "New York Crowd," for directing me to valuable resources on the Lincoln assassination, and for answering many questions I had in multiple conversations.

Eisenschiml's and Thomas's books are sold on Amazon. Kindle versions are available for all four of their books except *In the Shadow of Lincoln's Death*.

Regarding the so-called "Insurrection" at the Capitol on January 6, 2021, many conservatives were upset by the infiltration of the crowd by federal agents (estimated at over 200 by Congressman Clay Higgins)[1]; the media's mischaracterization of the event as ultraviolent, and compared to Pearl Harbor and 9/11 by Kamala Harris[2] (even though the only death on January 6 was an unarmed woman shot by a police officer); the government's suppression of video evidence that contradicted the narrative; and the imprisonment of over 800 people, most of whose only crime was being there. As we will see in analyzing the Lincoln assassination, such tactics aren't new, but have been occurring in America for more than a century and a half.

Notes

1. "Bombshell: 200 Undercover FBI Assets at US Capitol on Jan. 6, Congressman Estimates," *Association of Mature American Citizens*, January 10, 2024, https://tinyurl.com/yjyf8ee9.

2. Jake Lahut, "Kamala Harris Compares January 6 to Pearl Harbor and 9/11 in Anniversary Speech at the Capitol," *Business Insider*, January 6, 2022, https://tinyurl.com/5n7tmeha.

CHAPTER 1

THE MAINSTREAM NARRATIVE

Lincoln and Booth

First, let's refresh ourselves on the assassination's *official* story.
On April 9, 1865, General Robert E. Lee, commander of the
Army of Northern Virginia, surrendered to Union General Ulysses
S. Grant, effectively ending the Civil War (some Confederate
forces had not surrendered yet, but most soon would).

Five days later, on April 14 (Good Friday), President
Abraham Lincoln and his wife, Mary Todd, attended a comedy,

Our American Cousin, at Ford's Theatre in Washington, D.C. General Grant and his wife Julia were supposed to share the Presidential box with the Lincolns, but as Grant cancelled out that day, the Lincolns were accompanied by their acquaintances Major Henry Rathbone and his fiancée Clara Harris, daughter of U.S. Senator Ira Harris.

Henry Rathbone

At approximately 10:15 PM, shortly after the play's third act began, famed actor John Wilkes Booth entered the Presidential box and fired a bullet into the back of Lincoln's head at a moment the audience was roaring with laughter. Major Rathbone grappled with the assassin, but Booth stabbed him, inflicting a deep wound, and leaped from the box. Ironically, one of his spurs caught on the American flag draping the ledge, and he fell awkwardly to the stage below, breaking his leg. But this didn't prevent him from running, shouting "Sic semper tyrannis" ("thus always to tyrants") and "the South is avenged!" and escaping out the theater's rear. Most of the stunned audience did not immediately understand what had happened; Booth often performed at Ford's Theatre, and some thought he was even part of the act.

Booth and an accomplice, 22-year-old David Herold, rode horses south out of Washington. Meanwhile, the fatally wounded President was carried to a house across the street and laid on a bed.

At the same time as Lincoln's assassination, another of Booth's accomplices, Lewis Powell (also called Payne or Paine), a hulking Confederate veteran, entered the home of Secretary of State William Seward. Seward was bedridden, having been injured in a recent carriage accident. Powell ascended the stairs and was confronted by Seward's son Frederick. Powell drew a revolver; it misfired and he pistol-whipped the son until the latter collapsed. He then attacked Seward in his bed, stabbing him in the face and neck. Powell was restrained by Seward's male nurse, George Robinson, whom he stabbed; he also stabbed another of Seward's sons while escaping. The bloodied Secretary of State wasn't expected to live, but survived his wounds.

It was alleged that Booth's conspiracy had also planned to kill General Grant, Vice President Andrew Johnson, and other members of Lincoln's cabinet. Indeed, two days after the assassination, the Washington newspaper *The Intelligencer* declared: "We can state on the highest authority that it has been ascertained that there was a regular conspiracy to assassinate every member of the Cabinet, together with the Vice President." But only Lincoln and Seward were actually attacked.

Abraham Lincoln breathed his last at 7:22 AM. Secretary of War Edwin Stanton had already taken complete charge of the hunt for the assassins. That morning, Vice President Johnson was sworn in as the nation's Chief Executive.

In Maryland, Booth and Herold rode to the house of Dr. Samuel Mudd, a slight acquaintance of Booth. Mudd, knowing nothing yet of the assassination, treated Booth's leg. He made a makeshift cast for it, and had a neighbor construct crude crutches.

Booth and Herold continued their journey south. Booth's broken leg was worsening. After crossing into Virginia, they appealed to three Confederate soldiers, who assisted them to the farm of Richard Garrett, who let the pair sleep in his tobacco barn, not knowing their true identities.

On April 26 at night, a Union cavalry detachment tracked them to the farm. The soldiers surrounded the barn. Herold surrendered, but Booth refused to come out. The barn was set ablaze. Although the troops were under strict orders to bring the assassin back alive, one of the soldiers, Boston Corbett, fired at Booth through an opening in the barn, mortally wounding him. Booth was dragged out and died after about three hours. Corbett claimed he was guided by "divine providence."

As to Booth's co-conspirators, eight—real or alleged—were tried by a military rather than civil court. Four, including Powell, Herold, George Atzerodt (accused of planning to kill Vice President Johnson) and Mary Surratt (who owned a boardinghouse where

Booth sometimes met his accomplices) were hanged. Mrs. Surratt was the first woman to be executed by the United States.

The other four accused men, including Dr. Mudd, were sentenced to prison at hard labor.

It should be noted that Booth's initial plan had been to kidnap Lincoln, not assassinate him. Booth learned that on March 17, Lincoln was going to visit a hospital near the Soldiers' Home in Washington. Booth, Herold, Powell, Atzerodt, and three other conspirators—Samuel Arnold, Michael O'Laughlen, and John Surratt—waited on a deserted stretch of the road, planning to seize the President's carriage, abduct him, and take him south. Their hope was to create a bargaining chip for the Confederacy, whose fortunes were rapidly sinking. Specifically, they hoped to gain release of a large number of Southern POWs in exchange for Lincoln's return. However, Lincoln cancelled his plans to visit the hospital, and the plot failed.

(Although it's not a predominant feature of the mainstream narrative, I must interject that in March Booth also proposed to his accomplices that they kidnap the President during a performance at Ford's Theatre. Arnold, O'Laughlen and Surratt considered this idea absurd, and gradually abandoned Booth's circle.)

Allegedly, Booth changed his scheme from kidnapping to assassination after Lee's surrender, acting either out of vengeance, or perhaps the belief that, with Lincoln and his cabinet dead, the North would plunge into disarray, and the remaining Confederate forces in the South might rally again.

That's the official story. Now let's examine the holes.

CHAPTER 2

EARLY ANOMALIES IN THE ASSASSINATION STORY

Stanton's Behavior on April 14
Before the Assassination

One of the enduring questions is why, on the day of the assassination, Ulysses S. Grant decided to decline Lincoln's invitation to have the general and Mrs. Grant sit with him in the Presidential box. Grant's expected attendance was pre-announced, and is one reason Ford's Theatre was packed that evening—many people had observed Lincoln around Washington, but few had seen the general who had just defeated Lee, and were eager to catch a glimpse of him.

Officially, Grant gave as his reason his wish to visit family members in New Jersey, and indeed he and his wife were aboard a train for that purpose when Lincoln was shot. However, as Eisenschiml points out, there was no urgency to the family visit. No one in the family was ill. Grant could just as easily have taken the train the following morning, rather than refusing an invitation from his commander, the President of the United States.

Mainstream historians have claimed Grant failed to attend because of pressure from his wife, who didn't get along with Mary

Todd Lincoln. Few would deny that the President's wife was high-strung and temperamental. But there is little reason to believe that simply sitting with the Lincolns in a theater box, in full view of the public, would result in a disagreeable encounter between the two women.

There is another reason Grant declined. He went to the War Department that day and met with Secretary of War Edwin Stanton. As Eisenschiml notes, "All that is positively known is that Stanton immediately told him the presence of both the President and the lieutenant general at a public function would invite disaster. He urged Grant not to go to Ford's Theatre that night, and easily obtained his acquiescence."[1]

This sharply contrasts with Stanton's conduct toward Lincoln, who also visited the War Department that day. In earlier times, the President had been carefree about his safety. But recently he had received many death threats.

William Crook, who served as Lincoln's daytime bodyguard that day, wrote:

> I was surprised when, late on the afternoon of the 14th, I accompanied Mr. Lincoln on a hurried visit to the War Department, I found that the President was more depressed than I had ever seen him and his step unusually slow. … Mr. Lincoln said to me, "Crook, do you know, I believe there are men who want to take my life?" Then, after a pause, he said, half to himself, "And I have no doubt they will do it." The conviction with which he spoke dismayed me. I wanted to protest, but his tone had been so calm and sure that I found myself saying, instead, "Why do you think so, Mr. President?" "Other men have

been assassinated," was his reply.... . All I could say was, "I hope you are mistaken, Mr. President."[2]

Crook stood outside while Lincoln went into the War Department. David Homer Bates, in his memoir *Lincoln in the Telegraph Office*, says Stanton "urged the President to give up the theater-party."[3] He obviously did not urge him as persuasively as he had Grant. Bates put the onus on Lincoln, saying "Lincoln made light of all these signs [assassination threats],"[4] but this is clearly belied by the comments the President made to Crook.

Lincoln wanted a reliable bodyguard to accompany him to Ford's Theatre. He asked Stanton for the latter's aide, Major Thomas Eckert, who handled the cipher desk, to be his escort. Lincoln knew Eckert was a very strong officer; he had seen him break pokers over his arm. However, Stanton refused this request from his boss, saying he had important work for Eckert to do that evening.[5]

Stanton and Eckert

Lincoln even personally appealed to Eckert, suggesting that his work could wait until the morning. But Eckert also declined, citing his workload. It was quite unusual for a major to refuse a request from the nation's Commander in Chief. Disappointed but accommodating, Lincoln said he would take Major Rathbone instead, "but I should much rather have you, Major, since I know you can break a poker over your arm."[6]

Eisenschiml, in reviewing the government archives, discovered that Stanton and Eckert were *not* busy with evening work at the department.

> Apparently, neither Stanton nor Eckert, in spite of their assurances to Lincoln that they expected a busy evening, even put in an appearance at the War Department that night. Not a single wire went out from there signed by either of the men, and only two were received that were personally addressed to Stanton. But there is also direct evidence to show that Stanton, at least, did not even make a pretense of showing up at his office. According to the Secretary's own account of his experiences on the evening of the fourteenth of April, he went home and dined as usual. ... Now as to Eckert. Was he at his post during the hours when Lincoln had requested his protection against a possible assassin? He was not. The cipher department was left in charge of Mr. Bates [his assistant]; Eckert was not anywhere near there. Bates confirmed the report of a quiet evening, for he remembered nothing in particular that occurred prior to the assassination.[7]

Wiliam Crook accompanied the President back to the White House. Resuming his narrative:

> He said that Mrs. Lincoln and he, with a party, were going to the theatre to see Our American Cousin. "It has been advertised that we will be there," he said, "and I cannot disappoint the people. Otherwise I would not go. I do not want to go." I remember particularly that he said this, because it surprised me. The President's love for the theatre was well known. … So it seemed unusual to hear him say he did not want to go. When we had reached the White House and he had climbed the steps he turned and stood there a moment before he went in. Then he said, "Good-bye, Crook." It startled me. As far as I remember he had never said anything but "Good-night, Crook," before.[8]

Mainstream historians have attempted to justify Stanton's and Eckert's lying by claiming they did this to discourage Lincoln from going to Ford's Theatre. But if so, why didn't they relent once they saw Lincoln still planned to attend?

It's of interest that Bates and Crook clearly remembered Lincoln's April 14 visit to the War Department in their memoirs, both of which were published more than 40 years later. But in 1867, just two years later, testifying before the House Judiciary Committee, Stanton had no recollection of it. He said: "The order of Mr. Lincoln, of April 12, is on file in the War Department and was the last order he ever made, of which I have any knowledge. It was made the last time he was in the War Department."[9] Moments later, Stanton contradicted himself, saying, "On the day preceding his death ... Mr. Lincoln came over to the War Department."[10] But he still didn't recall the critical April 14th visit.

Worst Bodyguard Ever?

Replacing Crook, the bodyguard assigned to Lincoln that evening was John F. Parker, a member of Washington's Metropolitan Police Force.

John F. Parker (wore plainclothes when Lincoln's bodyguard)

He had an unsavory record, having been charged with misconduct for multiple reasons—being drunk on duty, falling asleep on duty, visiting a brothel, and using abusive language.[11] Not only did these charges not result in his dismissal, but he was one of four Metropolitan Police officers assigned to serve on Lincoln's bodyguard detail. On the fateful 14th, he showed up for duty three hours late.[12]

Initially he sat outside the President's box as he was supposed to. However, during the play's intermission, he left the theater, and went to the tavern next door, the Star Saloon. He was not at his post when Lincoln was shot, and did not show himself again until six o'clock the following morning. In a clumsy effort to salvage himself, he brought a streetwalker in to police headquarters, but amidst the assassination turmoil, she was not charged.[13] Although it isn't proven, some suspect he actually spent the night with the prostitute, since she wouldn't have likely been plying her trade on the street during the pandemonium.

Lincoln bodyguard William Crook stated that Parker should have been stationed at the rear of the President's box, "fully armed, and to permit no unauthorized person to pass . . . incredible as it may seem, he quietly deserted his post of duty … It was … through this guard's amazing recklessness—to use no stronger words—that Booth … accomplished his foul deed."[14]

One would think Parker would have been fired or even imprisoned for his conduct, which led to the President's murder. Although the Metropolitan Police initially charged Parker with neglect of duty, the charge was dropped, and no records remain as to why. This outcome must have required influence from someone with clout.

Not only did Parker keep his job with the Metropolitan Police, he remained on the Presidential bodyguard detail. On seeing him at the White House, Mary Todd Lincoln screamed that he was responsible for her husband's death.[15] Even allowing for her high-strung personality, no one can deny that she was right.

It has been suggested that he went to the saloon because Abraham Lincoln had excused him temporarily from his duties. However, this has no corroboration. No one in the Presidential box—Mrs. Lincoln, Major Rathbone, or his fiancée, mentioned hearing Lincoln say this. Furthermore, the concern Lincoln had expressed over his own safety, earlier that day, seemingly precludes that he was comfortable leaving himself unprotected.

The Metropolitan Police finally dismissed John Parker in August 1868. The charge? Sleeping on duty.[16] Why was he discharged for this relatively minor violation, but not for deserting his post as Lincoln's bodyguard? Might it be because Edwin Stanton had fallen from power in May 1868, and no longer had to be reckoned with?

Ned Spangler

A Contrast in Justice

While John Parker got off scot-free, others far less guilty were meted out savage punishment.

An example is affable Edman "Ned" Spangler, who worked at Ford's Theatre as a carpenter and helped shift scenery between acts. Spangler knew Booth, as the actor often performed there. But there is no evidence whatsoever that Spangler discussed assassinating the President with him, or was ever in contact with any of Booth's accomplices.

So what was Spangler's crime? On the evening of April 14, behind Ford's Theatre, Booth brought a horse he had hired from a stable. The stable's owner, John Pumphrey, had warned Booth that the horse was high-spirited and might break away. Booth therefore asked Spangler to hold the horse for him. Spangler, having no clue that Booth was about to shoot the President, briefly held on to the horse, but having work to do inside the theater, asked another Ford employee, Joseph "Peanut John" Burroughs, to hold the horse. That was it. That was the extent of Spangler's proven involvement. He made no attempt to hide himself after the assassination.

Secretary of War Edwin Stanton ordered Spangler's arrest. Awaiting trial by military tribunal, he, like the other accused, was placed in handcuffs and leg irons, and a canvas bag was placed over his head and tied at the neck, so that he couldn't hear well or see. The bag was kept in place at virtually all times. It had one small hole for breathing and eating, but was not taken off, even for meals. And with his arms shackled, Spangler couldn't feed himself. The guards, who were forbidden to speak to him, pitied him and fed him through the bag's hole.

All the other accused were forced to wear these bags except Mary Surratt, but she was still manacled. Every prisoner was confined to an isolated place, precluding communication with each other—or anyone else.

Stanton invented the wearing of these bags; it was unprecedented in Western criminal justice.

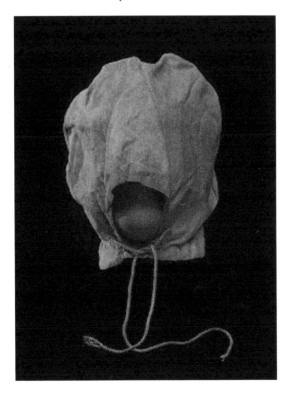

Spangler was not hanged, but sentenced to six years at hard labor. After more than four years, President Andrew Johnson commuted his sentence. Upon release, Spangler issued a public statement extensively detailing his innocence, which can be read at https://tinyurl.com/23nyedwt.

As we will see, this was not the only time in Lincoln assassination annals that justice was stood on its head, with the guilty going free while the innocent incurred merciless wrath.

Booth's derringer

Booth's Uncanny Confidence in His Plan

When John Wilkes Booth entered the Presidential box, he carried two weapons: a single-shot derringer pistol, and a knife.

Why was Booth so confident that he would only need one bullet to take out the President? All of Lincoln's bodyguards carried .38 Colt revolvers. Had John Parker, or another of Lincoln's more competent escorts, been at his post, he could have drawn his revolver and prevented Booth's entry.

As a knife is no match for a gun (except in the movie *The Magnificent Seven*), Booth might have been forced to use his one bullet to eliminate the bodyguard. Left with only a knife to dispose of Lincoln, he still would have had to first contend with Major Rathbone. With screams of "Help!" coming from the Presidential box, it would have likely swelled with rescuers before Booth could have finished off the President. That doesn't seem like much of a plan.

But let's say Booth intended to knife the bodyguard, preserving his single bullet for Lincoln. The struggle with the bodyguard probably would have been time-consuming, and he still would have had to battle Rathbone before reaching the President.

A better plan would have been approaching the box with a revolver. This would have been harder to conceal than the little derringer, but wearing a coat with deep pockets should have accomplished it.

Booth's confidence that he only needed one bullet to dispose of the President strongly suggests he had *foreknowledge that no bodyguard would be there.*

It should be added that while bodyguard John F. Parker was in the Star Saloon, Booth entered and braced himself with whiskey for the task ahead.[17] Whether the men spoke to each other is unknown.

Even if Booth spotted Parker, knew who he was, and realized Lincoln was without a bodyguard, it wouldn't have altered his strategy "spur of the moment"; Booth had planned carefully. He timed his shot to occur at the precise moment in the play when a lone actor was on stage, speaking a line that always drew roars of audience laughter—which would help drown out the sound of Booth's pistol.

Some have argued that Booth intended to deceive his way into the Presidential box, showing his card and, relying on his famous name, persuading any bodyguard that he only wanted to present his compliments to the President. But the time to "present his compliments" would have been during the intermission, not when the Lincolns were watching the ongoing performance. What guarantee would Booth have that such a ruse would succeed?

Booth's Selection of Targets

One of the first questions detectives ask when solving a crime: Who benefited from it?

Abraham Lincoln believed that, after the war, there should be national reconciliation. He opposed recriminations against the South. The Southern states that had seceded were to maintain voting rights, and their representatives restored to Congress in accord with the Constitution. This was Lincoln's vision of a "preserved Union."

However, the most hardcore members of his party, the "Radical Republicans," vehemently opposed Lincoln's plan. They wanted ranking Southern leaders hanged as traitors (although this wasn't done). Former Confederate officials were not to hold office. The Radical Republicans didn't want Southern states to regain representation in Congress. They knew that a combination of Southern and Northern Democrats would end the Republican stranglehold on power.

This is also primarily why Radical Republicans gave blacks the right to vote. It was not from simple humanitarianism. They knew that, in return for this right, most blacks would vote Republican, just as today's Democrats favor illegal immigration because they anticipate the immigrants will vote overwhelmingly Democrat.

Regarding all this, it must be understood that the Democratic and Republican parties of the 1860s bore little resemblance to their counterparts today. In those days, it was the Democrats who were conservative. The Radical Republicans were pro-Marxist, pro-totalitarian, and readily abused the Constitution. They have been portrayed as heroic for opposing slavery. But if they truly favored freedom, they would not have pushed through the Habeas Corpus Suspension Act of 1863. Under this act, the government imprisoned between 10,000 and 15,000 U.S. citizens without due process.[18] They were denied the right to trials and even to know the charges against them.

Following Lincoln's death, the Radical Republican plan of Reconstruction was imposed on the South. Its states were placed under martial law, run by appointed military officials (i.e., the War Department) rather than elected governors. 200,000 Federal troops occupied the South; martial law continued until 1877.

The war had destroyed the South's economy, with cities torched and crops destroyed. Although the South couldn't even pay its own war debt, it was compelled to help pay off the North's debt and even contribute to the pensions of Union soldiers. Thousands lost their homes due to onerous taxation; cotton was confiscated; exploitation by swarms of Northern carpetbaggers was devastating.

The Radical Republicans needed Lincoln to win reelection in November 1864, to keep their party in power. After that, he was expendable. In his second inaugural address (March 4, 1865),

Lincoln prescribed "malice toward none with charity for all"—the last words Radical Republicans wanted to hear.

Interestingly, John Wilkes Booth attended that inauguration and heard Lincoln speak those words. There is even an inauguration photo that shows both Lincoln speaking and Booth in the audience.

Neither the people of the South nor of the North benefited from Lincoln's death—only the Radical Republicans, and financiers who backed them. Their foremost spokesperson in the cabinet was Stanton, who called Lincoln "baboon"[19] and "the original gorilla."[20]

In an undisputed passage in his diary, Radical Republican Congressman George Julian described a caucus that took place on April 15, just hours after Lincoln was declared dead:

I like the radicalism of the members of this caucus, but have not in a long time heard so much profanity. It became intolerably disgusting. Their hostility towards Lincoln's policy of conciliation and contempt for his weakness were undisguised; and the universal feeling among radical men here is that his death is a godsend. It really seems so, for among the last acts of his official life was an invitation to some of the chief rebel conspirators to meet in Richmond and confer with us on the subject of peace.[21]

Lincon's murder brought no outbursts of rejoicing in the South. General Robert E. Lee condemned it. Confederate President Jefferson Davis said "it will be disastrous for our people."[22] Virginia newspapers called Booth a scoundrel. Sarah Morgan Dawson's 440-page *A Confederate Girl's Diary* closed with these words: "Our Confederacy has gone with one crash—the report of the pistol fired at Lincoln."[23]

All across the South, most people seemed to comprehend what the murder meant: the end of Lincoln's moderate plan of reconciliation, to be replaced by the harsh dictatorship of Reconstruction, made even worse by the South's being blamed for the assassination. Why did so many Southerners understand this, but not Booth?

As to William Seward, Eisenschiml notes: "The President and the Secretary of State were the two men in power whose program on reconstruction chiefly stressed conciliation."[24] David Cristy writes:

Like Lincoln, Seward had the same view of how to treat the South following the Civil War. He frequently defended his moderate reconciliation policy toward Southerners, enraging Radical Republicans who once regarded him as an ally.[25]

And Seward was the only man besides Lincoln against whom an actual assassination was tried on April 14, 1865. Of course, mainstream historians have cited other "attempts"—let's check these.

Notes

1. Otto Eisenschiml, *Why Was Lincoln Murdered?* (1937; reprint, London: Sothis Press, 2023), 61.
2. Wiliam H. Crook, *Through Five Administrations* (New York: Harper & Brothers, 1910), 65-66.
3. David Homer Bates, *Lincoln in the Telegraph Office* (New York: Century Co., 1907), 366.
4. Ibid.
5. Ibid., 367
6. Ibid., 367-68.
7. Eisenschiml, 37-38.
8. Crook, 67-68.
9. *Impeachment Investigation* (Washington, D. C.: Government Printing Office, 1868), 400.
10. Ibid.
11. Eisenschiml, 12-13.
12. Ronald G. Shafer, "The Night Lincoln Was Assassinated, His New Bodyguard Went Missing," *The Washington Post*, May 2, 2021, https://tinyurl.com/9n2xkz32.
13. Eisenschiml, 17.

14. William H. Crook, *Memories of the White House* (Boston: Little, Brown, 1911), 41-42.
15. Eisenschiml, 18.
16. Ibid., 19.
17. Statement of Peter Tartavul, co-owner of saloon; William C. Edwards and Edward Steers, eds., *The Lincoln Assassination: The Evidence* (Urbana: University of Illinois Press, 2009), Kindle edition, 1258.
18. David Greenberg, "Lincoln's Crackdown," *Slate*, November 30, 2001, https://tinyurl.com/y4s8wk74.
19. Crook, *Through Five Administrations*, 33.
20. Eisenschiml, 398.
21. "George W. Julian's Journal—the Assassination of Lincoln," *Indiana Magazine of History*, December 1915, 335.
22. Team Mighty, "How Did the South Feel about the Lincoln Assassination?" *We Are the Mighty*, September 29, 2023, https://tinyurl.com/yc3euprd.
23. Sarah Morgan Dawson, *A Confederate Girl's Diary* (Boston and New York: Houghton Mifflin, 1913), 440.
24. Eisenschiml, 173.
25. David Cristy, "'Higher Law' Seward," *Enid News and Eagle*, March 8, 2013, https://tinyurl.com/ys9ds6s2.

CHAPTER 3

ALLEGED BOTCHED ASSASSINATIONS

Secretary of War Edwin Stanton claimed he was "saved by the bell"—in this case a broken doorbell.

> I was tired out and went home early, and was in the back room playing with the children when the man came to my steps. If the door-bell had rung it would have been answered and the man admitted . . . but the bell-wire was broken a day or two before, and though we had endeavored to have it repaired, the bell-hanger had put it off because of a pressure of orders.[1]

Reportedly, this unidentified man shrank away into the darkness when other people approached, and was never seen again. And so ends the story of the attempt on Stanton's life. However, according to some who reported Lincoln's assassination to Stanton that night, the doorbell was in perfect working order.[2] And as Eisenschiml points out, would a repairman have kept an official as powerful as the Secretary of War waiting due to the pressure of *other* orders? Stanton's account was apparently just another "me too" story—"they tried to kill me too." Being an intended victim of the assassins would, of course, deflect suspicion from Stanton himself.

As to General Grant, the main substance of the claim of an assassination attempt is that his wife noticed a man staring at her while she was having lunch, and later that day, while the Grants were en route to the train station, she said she saw the same man riding alongside their carriage, peering at them. When Booth's picture appeared in the press, the Grants believed he was the man who followed their carriage. Later, Grant received an anonymous letter from someone who said he'd been hired to kill the general on the train, but had been obstructed by a locked door.[3] This individual was never identified and, as with Stanton, no actual assassination attempt occurred.

The Andrew Johnson story is more complicated. He was Lincoln's new Vice President, and having not yet established a Washington residence, was staying at a hotel, the Kirkwood House. George Atzerodt, one of Booth's accomplices in the Lincoln kidnapping plot, was instructed by Booth to take a room at the Kirkwood, which he did, the day before Lincoln's assassination. However, Booth had told Atzerodt to get an audience with Johnson—not to kill him, but to obtain passes to Richmond, which was now under Union control. Booth wanted the passes so that, when Lincoln visited Richmond, they could kidnap him in friendly Southern surroundings.

As we will see, the plot to assassinate Lincoln apparently did not originate until the day of the murder. Both Powell (who tried to kill Secretary of State Seward) and Atzerodt were not told of any murder plot until about two to three hours before Lincoln's assassination. Since the men weren't permitted to communicate with each other during the trial, but told the same story to detectives and attorneys, it is presumably true.

Powell, the rugged Confederate veteran, accepted the new mission of trying to assassinate Seward. In most accounts attributed to Atzerodt, he adamantly refused when Booth asked him to kill Vice President Johnson, and Booth didn't press the matter.

Atzerodt wasn't anyone's idea of an assassin, which Booth surely knew. German-born, he spoke broken English. He was known for lack of physical courage. His only role in the original kidnapping plot had been to take the abductors and Lincoln through southern areas of Maryland, which he knew well, and help them cross the Potomac River into Virginia in his boat.

Nevertheless, when detectives breached Atzerodt's room at the Kirkwood House, they found:

- a loaded Colt revolver
- a box of cartridges
- a Bowie knife
- a bankbook belonging to John Wilkes Booth
- a handkerchief marked "Mary Booth," Booth's mother
- a coat belonging to David Herold, Booth's riding partner
- a handkerchief marked "H. M. Nelson," Herold's sister
- a war map of the Southern states
- a spur

As Eisenschiml notes, this was a detective's dream come true. But whether Atzerodt intended to assassinate Johnson or not, why would he leave behind a mountain of incriminating evidence in his hotel room? And if he was planning to kill the Vice President, why did he sign the hotel register using his real name?

This evidence (if we can truly call it that) was paramount in hanging Atzerodt; no one seemed interested in inquiring if he might have been framed. As Eisenschiml notes, the spur seems to have been left almost as a comic touch, indicating that the murderers planned to escape on horseback rather than by coach, train, or boat.

A controversial aspect of the Johnson case is that Booth himself attempted to call on the Vice President late on the morning of April 14. Johnson wasn't in, and Booth left a card for him that said:

> Don't wish to disturb you. Are you at home?
> J. Wilkes Booth

The card has been preserved to this day. Here it is:

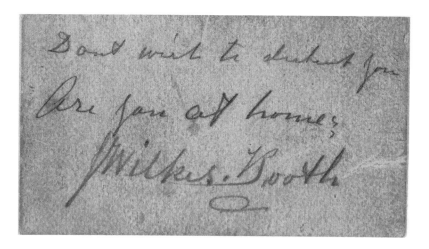

Mainstream historians usually have two explanations for this card. One is that Booth planned to assassinate Johnson right then and there. But this cannot be. If Booth had killed Johnson that morning, Lincoln—the prime target—would not have gone to Ford's Theatre that evening, but would have been kept under heavy guard. The second explanation advanced is that Booth and Johnson were *colluding*. Indeed, when Johnson later fell out of favor with the Radical Republicans (because he was less harsh on the South than they had hoped), they attempted to impeach him. Part of their strategy was to accuse Johnson of conspiring to kill Lincoln, and they used this card as "proof."

However, M. B. Ruggles, one of the three Confederate soldiers who accompanied Booth to the Garrett farm, rendered a much different explanation. He discussed the assassination with Booth at length. Booth told him there had never been a plan to kill Johnson, and that Atzerodt—who was later hanged—knew nothing about assassination. Ruggles related: "That Andrew Johnson might appear to be implicated in the plot of assassination, Booth said that he had left that morning a note at the hotel where the Vice-President lived, to compromise him."[4] If this was Booth's intent, it worked, since the Radical Republicans later used the card when attempting to impeach Johnson. Eisenschiml observed: "This is an astounding revelation; for what sense was there in Booth's trying to throw suspicion on a dead Johnson?"[5]

Notes

1. Frank Abial Flower, *Edwin McMasters Stanton* (Akron, Ohio; New York: Saalfield Publishing, 1905), 279.
2. Otto Eisenschiml, *In the Shadow of Lincoln's Death* (New York: Wilfred Funk, 1940), 359.
3. Horace Porter, *Campaigning with Grant* (New York: The Century Co., 1907), 498-500.

4. Prentiss Ingraham, "Pursuit and Death of John Wilkes Booth," *The Century* (January 1890), 445.
5. Otto Eisenschiml, *Why Was Lincoln Murdered?* (1937; reprint, London: Sothis Press, 2023), 171.

CHAPTER 4

STANTON'S BEHAVOR IMMEDIATELY FOLLOWING THE ASSASSINATION

■ On the evening of the 14th, Stanton proceeded to the dying President's bedside, and put himself in charge of the murder investigation. This was itself questionable. John Wilkes Booth was a civilian; he had shot a civilian President in a civilian environment. Normally this would have fallen under the Attorney General's jurisdiction—but Stanton advanced a theory (subsequently discredited) that the Confederate government had ordered the assassination; that it was therefore an act of war and came under the War Department (the equivalent of today's Defense Department). Stanton then became virtual dictator of the United States, while Andrew Johnson, who had barely gotten his feet wet as Lincoln's new Vice President, uncomfortably assumed the role of Chief Executive.

■ As Secretary of War, Stanton had already placed the nation's telegraph service under War Department control. This gave him a monopoly on what was then the country's most advanced communications system. The man directly in charge of it was his assistant, Major Thomas Eckert. Stanton and Eckert were the two men who, under a false pretext, denied Lincoln the protection he wanted at Ford's Theatre.

Eckert's loyalty to Stanton didn't hurt his career. He subsequently became Assistant Secretary of War, and after leaving the government, experienced a meteoric rise in the telegraph industry, culminating with his becoming president and chairman of Western Union. One doesn't usually attain such positions without powerful backing.

As Eisenschiml notes, "A bizarre incident on the night of April 14 was an interruption of all telegraphic services between Washington and the outside world, lasting about two hours."[1]

Two years later, the House of Representatives Judiciary Committee asked Eckert about this:

Q. Did you have knowledge of the telegraph lines at or about the time of the assassination of President Lincoln?

A. I did.

Q. Was there any interruption of the lines that night?

A. Yes, sir.

Q. What was it?

A. It was my impression at the time they were cut, but we got circuit again very early the next morning. The manager of the Commercial office reported the cause to have been crossing of wires in main batteries. Throwing a ground wire over the main wires would have caused the same trouble, and taking it off would have put it in ordinary working condition.

Q. Was there an investigation into what was the real cause of the difficulty?

A. No, sir. It did not at the time seem to be sufficiently important, as the interruption only continued about two hours. I was so full of business of almost every character that I could not give it my personal attention. The interruption was only of a portion of the lines between Washington and Baltimore. We worked our City Point line all the time.

Q. Do you know whether the Commercial lines were interrupted at that time?

A. Yes, sir. It was only the Commercial lines that were interrupted; it was in the Commercial office and not in the War Department office. I could not ascertain with certainty what the facts were without making a personal investigation, and I had not the time to do that.[2]

Eckert's 1867 testimony, that only a portion of traffic to Baltimore was interrupted, contradicted what the press had reported in 1865. George A. Townsend wrote in the May 2 *New York World*: "Within fifteen minutes after the murder, the wires were severed entirely around the city, excepting only a secret wire for government uses, which leads to Old Point. I am told that by this wire the government reached the fortifications around Washington, first telegraphing all the way to Old Point, and then back to the outlying forts. This information comes to me from so many creditable channels that I must concede it."[3]

Although Eckert attempted to dismiss the issue as "no big deal," if the problem was as extensive as first reported, it was *very* important, because it gave the murderers a two-hour head start before news of the assassination was communicated. That the lines were not physically cut suggests that someone with professional expertise caused the disruption. No one in Booth's circle had that expertise; Eckert did. Perhaps Stanton wasn't entirely lying when he told Lincoln he had work for Eckert that night—which he couldn't very well do at Ford's Theatre. I have no proof against Eckert, but will just leave it there.

Eisenschiml observes that Eckert pleaded that he couldn't investigate the matter because he was *too busy*—the same excuse he had untruthfully given Lincoln when refusing to escort him at Ford's Theatre. Yet Eckert was in charge of the nation's telegraph services—what could have been more important than their proper functioning during the assassination's aftermath?

- There was never any question that John Wilkes Booth, an extremely well-known figure, was Lincoln's assassin. By midnight, 17 persons had already identified Booth as the killer at police headquarters,[4] and several more identified him to investigators at the Petersen house, where Stanton was beside the dying Lincoln.

Corporal James Tanner took shorthand notes of the witness statements at the Petersen house. In a letter written two days later, he said: "In fifteen minutes I had testimony enough down to hang Wilkes Booth, the assassin, higher than ever Haman hung."[5]

Yet after telegraph service was restored around midnight, Stanton failed to reveal Booth's name in dispatches until after 3AM, when newspapers had begun printing their morning editions. This gave Booth extra hours of escape time before his identification became widely known.

- Then there was the anomalous sequence of troop deployments to intercept the assassin(s). The War Department notified troops to the north first. This made little sense. Booth and any accomplices weren't likely to ride north, where they would find no refuge and Booth was very recognizable. Canada was more than 400 miles away.

Next deployed were soldiers west of Washington. This area was also a highly improbable direction for Booth, as it was thick with Federal troops.

Last to be deployed were troops to the south, the conspirators' obvious destination. At 4 AM, Stanton closed all southern exits leading out of Washington. But this accomplished nothing, as Booth was already 30 miles south, and would have undoubtedly gotten further if uninjured.[6] Eisenschiml notes:

> Only one hole was left in the network that Stanton had spun around the nation's Capital. This was the road that pointed straight south from Washington to Port Tobacco. It was the road Booth was most likely to use; for it led toward the Confederacy, the only place where the assassin could hope to find protection. In all the wires sent out from the War Department during the night of April 14, this route was not mentioned once and no precautions were taken to guard it. The only road that Stanton failed to bar was the one by which Booth escaped from Washington; and there never should have been the slightest doubt that he would use it.[7]

Notes

1. Otto Eisenschiml, *Why Was Lincoln Murdered?* (1937; reprint, London: Sothis Press, 2023), 78.
2. *Impeachment Investigation* (Washington, D. C.: Government Printing Office, 1868), 673.
3. Eisenschiml, 78.
4. Ibid., 68.
5. William E. Barton, *The Life of Abraham Lincoln*, vol. II (1925; reprint, Boston: Books, Inc., 1943), 472.
6. Eisenschiml, 94.
7. Ibid., 96.

CHAPTER 5

IN PURSUIT OF
JOHN WILKES BOOTH

Big money was offered for capturing the alleged assassins. $50,000 in 1865 is over a million dollars today. These rewards somewhat hampered the investigation, because people were competing for the money and often didn't wish to share information. As we'll see, John Surratt, for whom $25,000 was offered, had nothing to do with the assassination and was proven to be in Elmira, New York, 300 miles away, at the time.

After having his broken leg attended to by Dr. Mudd, and spending a few hours at the doctor's home to rest, Booth departed with Herold. The two made their way to the farm of Samuel Cox, a Southern sympathizer who lived near the Potomac River. Cox wouldn't let them stay in his house, but allowed them to remain in a nearby pine thicket for several days, bringing them food and newspapers, until squadrons of Union cavalry had finished passing. With help from Cox's stepbrother, Thomas Jones, they procured a small rowboat, eventually making their way across the Potomac into Virginia. There Booth threw himself on the mercy of three young Confederate officers, who guided him and

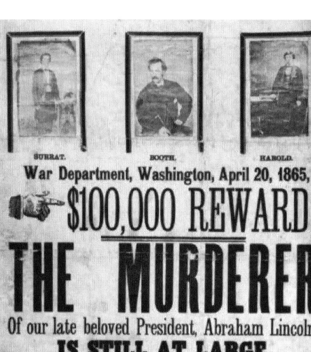

SURRAT.   BOOTH.   HAROLD.

War Department, Washington, April 20, 1865,

$100,000 REWARD!

THE MURDERER

Of our late beloved President, Abraham Lincoln,

IS STILL AT LARGE.

$50,000 REWARD

Will be paid by this Department for his apprehension, in addition to any reward offered by Municipal Authorities or State Executives.

$25,000 REWARD

Will be paid for the apprehension of JOHN H. SURRATT, one of Booth's Accomplices.

$25,000 REWARD

Will be paid for the apprehension of David C. Harold, another of Booth's accomplices.

LIBERAL REWARDS will be paid for any information that shall produce to the arrest of either of the above-named criminals, or their accomplices.

All persons harboring or secreting the said persons, or either of them, or aiding or abiding their concealment or escape, will be treated as accomplices in the murder of the President and the attempted assassination of the Secretary of State, and shall be subject to trial before a Military Commission and the punishment of DEATH.

Let the stain of innocent blood be removed from the land by the arrest and punishment of the murderers.

All good citizens are exhorted to aid public justice on this occasion. Every man should consider his own conscience charged with this solemn duty, and rest neither night nor day until it be accomplished.

EDWIN M. STANTON, Secretary of War.

DESCRIPTIONS.—BOOTH is Five Feet 7 or 8 inches high, slender build, high forehead, black hair, black eyes, and wears a heavy black moustache.

JOHN H. SURRAT is about 5 feet, 9 inches. Hair rather thin and dark; eyes rather light; no beard. Would weigh 145 or 150 pounds. Complexion rather pale and clear, with color in his cheeks. Wore light clothes of fine quality. Shoulders square; cheek bones rather prominent; chin narrow; ears projecting at the top; forehead rather low and square, but broad. Parts his hair on the right side; neck rather long. His lips are firmly set. A slim man.

DAVID C. HAROLD is five feet six inches high, hair dark, eyes dark, eyebrows rather heavy, full face, nose short, hand short and fleshy, feet small, instep high, round bodied, naturally quick and active, slightly closes his eyes when looking at a person.

NOTICE.—In addition to the above, State and other authorities have offered rewards amounting to almost one hundred thousand dollars, making an aggregate of about TWO HUNDRED THOUSAND DOLLARS.

Herold to Richard Garrett's farm. They told Garrett that Booth was a wounded Confederate soldier.

Provost Marshal James O'Beirne, later a Congressional Medal of Honor recipient for valor during the Civil War, was commanding a squad of detectives pursuing Booth and Herold. O'Beirne reported that he was close to capturing the pair, but was ordered to remain where he was.

James O'Beirne

In remarks dated December 27, 1865, O'Beirne stated, with apparent irony:

> In obedience to orders subsequently asked by me from the Secretary of War, I returned to Washington after Booth and Harold had been discovered a short distance beyond where I pursued them. I repaired at once in person to the Honorable Secretary of War. I was by him warmly congratulated and complimented during my interview with him in the hallway of the 1st floor War Department Building. He spoke in words and substance as follows: "You have done your duty nobly and you have the satisfaction of knowing that if you did not succeed in capturing Booth, it was, at all events, certainly the information which you gave that led to it."[1]

Left to right:
Luther Baker,
Lafayette Baker,
Everton Conger

Why didn't Stanton let O'Beirne complete his mission and capture Booth and Herold? Instead, at the cost of an extra day's time, a cavalry detachment was sent from Washington: 26 soldiers under the command of Lieutenant Edward Doherty. Two other officers were attached to that command. One was Lieutenant Luther Baker, the cousin of Lafayette Baker—one of Stanton's right-hand men in the War Department, and head of the National Detective Bureau (later called the Secret Service), where he acquired a reputation for ruthlessness and personal corruption. The other officer was Lieutenant Colonel Everton Conger, an ex-serviceman now a detective in Lafayette Baker's service. Largely due to his rank, Conger was nominally in command of the cavalry detachment, though he was no longer on active military duty.

As we've noted, on the final
night at the Garrett farm barn,
David Herold surrendered, but
Booth refused. The barn was
set ablaze, and, against official
orders, he was shot and mortally
wounded. The tobacco barn had
open slats making it possible to
see in and out.

There are problems with the
scenario. I always thought it odd
that a cavalry detachment was
too timid to simply enter the barn
and rush Booth. He was injured, and

Boston Corbett

outnumbered nearly 30 to one. Granted, he might have gotten off
a couple of shots before being overtaken, but surely Union cavalry
had faced greater challenges during the Civil War.

Another option would have been to simply wait Booth out.
How long would he last without food or water?

It is also questionable if Boston Corbett really fired the fatal
shot. Not one soldier in the detachment reported observing him
shoot. The only witness ever to support it was R. B. Garrett, a son
of the farm's owner. Garrett, then twelve years old, told the story
to a Baltimore newspaper more than 30 years later.[2] Could a child
have been mistaken about the shooter's identity, especially in the
dark? Did he hear Corbett's name spoken that night, or was he
later just repeating the name he'd read in newspaper accounts?

Lieutenant Baker thought Lt. Colonel Conger shot Booth.
Before the House Judiciary Committee, he testified:

I supposed, at the time, that Conger shot him, and I said, "What on earth did you shoot him for?" Said he, "I did not shoot him." Then the idea flashed on my mind that if he did, it had better not be known.[3]

The lethal shot, which pierced Booth's neck and paralyzed him, ensured he would never talk. This further exchange occurred between Baker and the Committee:

> Q. Do you know any reason why you were not called as a witness on the conspiracy trial?
>
> A. I do not. I expected to be. I was summoned as a witness, but was informed, after I got here, that I was not wanted.
>
> Q. Was there any reason assigned?
>
> A. None; and I was very much surprised at it.[4]

Baker accompanied Booth's body back to Washington, where he made a full report to Joseph Holt, Judge Advocate General of the Union Army. Holt later became chief prosecutor at the conspiracy trial. Interestingly, Baker's statement disappeared from the War Department's files—a fate, which, as we will see, befell many key documents pertaining to the Lincoln assassination. Here is more testimony Baker gave before the Judiciary Committee:

> A. I gave my statement to Judge Holt, on the gunboat, before I gave up charge of the body.
>
> Q. Were you sworn on the trial of Mrs. Surratt?
>
> A. I was not. My testimony has never been taken, except before Judge Holt, and that has been disposed of.

Q. What do you mean by that?

A. It cannot be found. I was the first who gave any
evidence in the case. General Baker took me
down into the cabin of the gunboat, and I gave my
evidence to Judge Holt. Colonel Conger was present
and assented to its truth.

Q. Was it a sworn statement?

A. It was.

Q. When was it taken?

A. The morning I came up with the body.

Q. Did Judge Holt keep your testimony?

A. He did. I suppose it went on the files, but when the
subject was up before the Committee of Claims in
relation to the distribution of rewards, it could not
be found. ...

Q. You do not know what has become of that
testimony?

A. My opinion is that there has been some foul
play about it.

Q. What do you mean?

A. I think it has been destroyed. My impression is that
it was destroyed in order to suppress the facts which
it proved as to my having charge of the party, so
that my claim to the chief share of the reward would
not be so good.

Q. How much of the reward did you get?

A. Three thousand dollars.

Q. How much did Conger get?

A. Fifteen thousand dollars.[5]

Baker was correct here. The $50,000 reward for Booth's apprehension was divided among many individuals. But although it was originally announced that Baker and Conger would receive $4,000 each,[6] their roles in the expedition having been quite comparable, Baker's share was eventually reduced to $3,000 and Conger's raised exponentially to $15,000.

Baker's lost statement to Holt evidently resurfaced, and can now be found on pages 128 to 137 of *The Lincoln Assassination: The Rewards File*, complied by William C. Edwards. But interestingly, the section where Baker ran into the barn and viewed Booth's body is "crossed off," a polite way of saying "redacted."

Boston Corbett, who originally said he had been guided by "divine providence," later changed his story, claiming Booth was aiming a carbine at him or at another of the soldiers;[7] i.e., Corbett said he shot Booth in self-defense. This seems unlikely, however, since the lethal bullet traversed Booth's neck from side to side—he was not facing whoever shot him. If Booth had actually started shooting, self-defense might have been a justifiable motive, but since he didn't, violating the strict order to bring Booth back alive was inexcusable.

Another issue: Everyone who heard the shot described it as a pistol shot. As Don Thomas writes:

> According to a 1965 *Civil War Times Magazine* article, "Album of the Lincoln Murder," p. 45, Research Consultant Colonel Julian E. Raymond uncovered evidence that Corbett had only a carbine when Booth was shot. The revolver Corbett is wearing in the Library of Congress photograph, pictured on the magazine page 45, is a pistol issued to him only after Booth died.[8]

Corbett was sent to Washington to be court-martialed for disobeying orders. However, Secretary of War Stanton simply dismissed the charges, saying, "The rebel is dead—the patriot lives. He has saved us continued excitement, delay and expense—the patriot is released."[9] Stanton neglected to mention that cancelling the court-martial also prevented a meticulous investigation of what really happened at the Garrett farm.

Notes

1. Otto Eisenschiml, *Why Was Lincoln Murdered?* (1937; reprint, London: Sothis Press, 2023), 128.
2. Hamilton Gay Howard, *Civil War Echoes* (Washington, D.C.: Howard Publishing, 1907), 98.
3. *Impeachment Investigation* (Washington, D. C.: Government Printing Office, 1868), 481.
4. Ibid., 483.
5. Ibid., 483, 486.
6. William C. Edwards, ed., *The Lincoln Assassination: The Rewards File* (2012), 17, https://tinyurl.com/2mw93hcr.
7. *The Assassination of President Lincoln and the Trial of the Conspirators*, comp. Benn Pitman (New York: Moore, Wilstach & Baldwin, 1865), 94.
8. Don Thomas, "Evidence Does Not Support a Confederate Conspiracy to Kill Lincoln," 23, https://tinyurl.com/mtu4ad8k.
9. Byron Berkeley Johnson, *Abraham Lincoln and Boston Corbett* (Waltham, Mass.: 1914), 37-38.

CHAPTER 6

WAS BOOTH THE MAN IN THE BARN?

This has perhaps become the most controversial Lincoln assassination subject. Many have said another man was killed at Garrett's farm, and that John Wilkes Booth lived for years afterwards under another name. *Multiple* theories have been advanced about who Booth became. I don't plan to vet them all here.

Operating nearly 100 years apart, both Otto Eisenschiml and Don Thomas investigated these claims at length. Both believed the preponderance of evidence favors Booth dying at Garrett's farm.

From the time Booth and Herold left Dr. Samuel Mudd's home on April 15, to the Garrett farm confrontation on April 26, the pair's course can be tracked daily, and their descriptions were consistently described by those who saw them, fed them, sheltered them, and/or helped them with transport—including Samuel Cox and his stepbrother Thomas Jones; John J. Hughes; Elizabeth Queensbury; Dr. Richard Stuart; William L. Byant; the three Confederate soldiers (Mortimer Ruggles, Absalom Bainbridge, and Willie Jett) who brought them to the Garrett farm); the Garretts themselves; and others. Ruggles noted that "his wounded leg was greatly swollen, inflamed, and dark, as from bruised blood, while it seemed to have been wretchedly dressed, the splints being simply pasteboard rudely tied about it. That he suffered intense pain all the time there was no doubt, though he tried to conceal his agony, both physical and mental."[1]

(Dr. Mudd had predicted that if Booth kept riding, the leg would swell and require additional treatment.[2]) Ruggles also conversed with Booth at length about the assassination.

On April 25th, the Conger-Baker-Doherty detachment rode past the Garrett farm, and Booth and Herold were advised to hide in the woods. The cavalry was tracking down one of the three Confederates who had been identified as helping Booth—Willie Jett, who had gone to visit his girlfriend in Bowling Green. Later, Booth and Herold, thinking the danger had passed and that there would be no trouble at night, returned from the woods and were told they could sleep in Garrett's tobacco barn. This would prove their undoing. The cavalry captured Jett, who, under threat of death, led the detachment to the Garrett farm at 2 AM.

All the interaction between Booth and the Union soldiers was characteristic of Booth. When Herold surrendered, Booth shouted that the young man was innocent. Looking through the barn's slats, the soldiers could see Booth hobbling on a crutch. He had a carbine and two pistols—the same weaponry he and Herold had picked up at a Maryland tavern on their night of escape from Washington, and which witnesses saw them with during their journey.

After Booth was mortally wounded, some items removed from his person could only have belonged to him—such as his diary, and a diamond stickpin he was known to carry, engraved "Dan Bryant to J. W. Booth." (Dan Bryant was an actor friend of

Booth's.) It takes a few gymnastics of explanation to put them in another man's hands.

Some contend that Booth escaped the barn and was replaced by someone else. But in great pain, his broken leg swelling, Booth had severely limited mobility. Perhaps the most popular theory as to who replaced Booth: James William Boyd, whom even *Wikipedia* discusses in this context. However, as Don Thomas points out, at age 42 and standing 6 foot 2, Boyd would have made a poor double for Booth, who was 26 and 5 foot 8.

After Booth's death, his corpse was wrapped and sewn in an Army blanket, and transported by wagon, then steamer to the Washington Navy Yard, where it was placed on the ironclad *USS Montauk* at 1:45 AM on April 27. In all, transportation took some 19 hours.

On the *Montauk*, an inquest was held later on the 27th to identify the body and determine cause of death. This has also been a source of controversy. Let's examine both sides. Surgeon General Joseph K. Barnes, Dr. Joseph Janvier Woodward, and Dr. George Brainard Todd performed the autopsy.

Besides confirming the cause of death was a bullet that passed laterally through the neck, the following points tended to confirm the body as being Booth's:

- Surgeon General Barnes reported: "The left leg and foot were encased in an appliance of splints and bandages, upon the removal of which, a fracture of the fibula (small bone of the leg) 3 inches above the ankle joint, accompanied by considerable ecchymosis [small bruises from broken blood vessels], was discovered."[3] This was consistent with Booth's leg injury.

▪ Dr. John Frederick May, who had once removed a tumor from the back of Booth's neck, identified the scar from that operation, although (as we will see) he also expressed hesitancy about the corpse being Booth.

▪ Dr. William Merrill, Booth's dentist, is said to have identified two gold fillings he had made for the actor,[4] but it appears that no official report from Merrill is in the records.

▪ Booth's sister Asia said: "He had perfectly shaped hands, and across the back of one he had clumsily marked, when a little boy, his initials in India ink."[5] This had the effect of a tattoo and stayed with Booth for life. On the *Montauk*, the tattoo was identified by Charles Dawson, a clerk at Washington's National Hotel, where Booth often stayed; Dawson said he had frequently noticed the tattoo.[6] It was also recalled by Marine Sergeant John Peddicord, who was ordered to stand watch over the body on the *Montauk*.[7] And Absalom Bainbridge, one of the three Confederate soldiers who took Booth to Garrett's farm, recalled: "Over his shoulders drooped a long gray shawl, which he said had served him well in covering the telltale initials 'J.W.B.' done in Indian ink on his right hand. These letters he showed to us to establish his identity."[8]

Initially, Booth's corpse was unceremoniously buried in a publicly undisclosed location at the Old Penitentiary in Washington. In 1869, President Andrew Johnson ordered the remains returned to the Booths. The corpse was viewed by several members of the Booth family, Booth's friends John and Henry Ford, and again, it is said, by his dentist William Merrill. There was a consensus that it was John Wilkes Booth; the body was buried in an unmarked grave at the Booth family plot.[9]

Criticisms have also been leveled against the above findings.

- Dr. John Frederick May, who identified Booth's surgical scar, initially thought the corpse wasn't Booth, according to a statement he made in 1887:

> The cover was removed, and to my great astonishment revealed a body in whose lineaments there was to me no resemblance of the man I had known in life! My surprise was so great that I at once said to General Barnes, "There is no resemblance in that corpse to Booth, nor can I believe it to be that of him." After looking at it for a few moments, I asked "Is there a scar upon the back of its neck?" He replied "There is." I then said, "If that *is* the body of Booth, let me describe the scar before it is seen by me"; and did so as to its position, its size, and its general appearance, so accurately as caused him to say "You have described the scar as well as if you were looking at it; and it looks, as you have described it, more like the cicatrix of a burn than that made by a surgical operation." The body being then turned, the back of the neck was examined, and my *mark* was unmistakably found by me upon it. And it being afterwards, at my request, placed in a sitting position, standing, and looking down upon it, I was finally enabled to imperfectly recognize the features of Booth. But never in a human being had a greater change taken place, from the man whom I had seen in the vigor of life and health, than in that of the haggard corpse which was before me, with its yellow and discolored skin; its unkempt and matted hair; and its whole facial

expression sunken and sharpened by the exposure and starvation it had undergone![10]

Casting further doubts was Dr. May's recollection that the corpse's fracture was of the right leg.[11] But given that he wrote this more than 20 years after the fact, the immediate inquest should carry greater weight. In his final analysis, May wrote: "But the mark made by the scalpel during life remained indelible in death, and settled beyond all question at the time, and all cavil in the future, the identity of the man who had assassinated the President."[12]

- The identification of Booth's corpse by family and friends has also been criticized. It was done informally, unsworn, and took place about four years after Booth's death, by which time much decay had occurred. Why, some inquire, were people very close to Booth not asked to identify him at the inquest, such as family and friends—surely they would have known him better than the National Hotel's desk clerk. However, availability—geographic distance and the fact that some of Booth's friends had been jailed on suspicion—should be factored in.

Finally, Edwin Stanton had the body photographed at the time of autopsy. The picture was given to Stanton, but never published. This raises the question if the photo would have cast doubt on the corpse being Booth. There might be another explanation, however. Possibly Stanton never intended publishing the photo—he may have only wanted to make absolutely sure, for himself, that his underlings had really eliminated Booth, and not hastily substituted another corpse in order to collect reward money. Stanton wanted to sleep nights again. And if rumors later circulated that

Booth was still alive, leading people on wild goose chases instead of investigating Washington, that probably suited Stanton fine.

Of the $50,000 bounty that was placed on Booth's head, $15,000 went to Lt. Colonel Conger, and only $3,000 to Lieutenant Baker, as we've noted. This made little sense, as the two men played comparable roles in tracking down and confronting Booth. Might it relate to Baker's belief that Conger shot Booth?

Regarding Booth being in the barn, and the corpse brought to Washington, I acknowledge that arguments exist on both sides of this controversy, but I concur with Eisenschiml and Thomas that the bulk of evidence favors Booth being killed, as said. Edwin Stanton owed Booth nothing. He initially seemed eager to let Booth escape as "the man who knew too much." But the unanticipated broken leg slowed the assassin down, and once his capture became inevitable, murdering him became the best means of silencing him.

I may be wrong, of course, and I leave the door open to alternative interpretations.

Notes

1. Prentiss Ingraham, "Pursuit and Death of John Wilkes Booth," *The Century* (January 1890), 444.
2. Statement of Samuel Mudd; William C. Edwards and Edward Steers, eds., *The Lincoln Assassination: The Evidence* (Urbana: University of Illinois Press, 2009), Kindle edition, 941.
3. "John Wilkes Booth's Autopsy," *Abraham Lincoln's Assassination*, https://rogerjnorton.com/Lincoln83.html.
4. Todd Van Beck, "The Burials of John Wilkes Booth," *American Funeral Director*, April 2020, https://tinyurl.com/yeyk784n.

5. Eleanor Farjeon, *The Unlocked Book: A Memoir of John Wilkes Booth by His Sister Asia Booth Clarke* (New York: G. P. Putnam's Sons, 1938), 59.

6. Otto Eisenschiml, *In the Shadow of Lincoln's Death* (New York: Wilfred Funk, 1940), 36.

7. Ibid., 37.

8. Ingraham, 444.

9. "John Wilkes Booth's Autopsy"; Van Beck.

10. John Frederick May, "The Mark of The Scalpel," *Records of the Columbia Historical Society* (1910), 55, https://tinyurl.com/53ma838a.

11. Ibid.

12. Ibid., 56.

CHAPTER 7
THE LAW GETS PERVERTED

As to Booth's accomplices—real or alleged—eight people were tried. In accordance with Stanton's wishes, they were judged by a military commission rather than a civilian court. This meant they were denied the Constitutional right to trial by jury. They faced nine military officers, most with no legal experience, and all handpicked by Stanton, who was their boss. A majority of five "guilty" votes was sufficient to convict, whereas a jury verdict had to be unanimous. And six military votes was enough to impose a death sentence.

As we mentioned in Ned Spangler's case, all the accused prisoners were kept handcuffed, with their legs manacled, in total isolation. All except Mary Surratt were required to keep canvas bags over their heads, tied at the neck. The guards were not allowed to speak to them.

In 1902, Samuel Arnold, the last survivor of the accused, described his incarceration:

> The covering for the head was made of canvas, which
> covered the entire head and face, dropping down in front
> to the lower portion of the chest. It had cords attached,
> which were tied around the neck and body in such a

manner that to remove it was a physical impossibility. It was frequently impossible to place food in my mouth. No doubt Stanton wished to accustom me to the death cap before execution. … It being with the greatest difficulty, and frequently impossible, to place food in my mouth, a sentinel kindly volunteering his services to perform that office for me.[1]

Later, an even crueler hood was devised. Again quoting Arnold:

I found that a differently constructed hood had been prepared for a head cover of a much more tortuous and painful pattern than the one formerly used. It fitted the head tightly, containing cotton pads, which were placed directly ever the eyes, having the tendency to push the eyeballs far back in the sockets. One small aperture was about the nose through which to breathe, and one by which food could be served to the mouth … . The cords were drawn as tight as the jailor in charge could pull them, causing the most excruciating pain and suffering, and then tied in such a manner around the neck that it was impossible to remove them.[2]

The *Columbia Law Review* notes that "at the outset of trial the defendants were paraded before the commission 'with black linen masks covering all their faces except tip of nose and mouth, heavily chained and each led staggering and clanking in, by his keeper. It was a horrid sight.'" The *Review* also notes that "the accused were not offered counsel until after they were arraigned before the commission, and for some only the day before testimony began, with no time to prepare for trial."[3]

The defense attorneys were almost never permitted to speak with their clients in private—only in the courtroom, with the defendants beside their guards, and surrounded by a crowd, whispering through the bars of the dock.[4] During the trial, defendants weren't allowed to speak on their own behalf. And they remained shackled in the courtroom. Congressman A. J. Rogers said:

> Since the trial of Cranbourne, in 1696 . . . no prisoner has ever been tried in irons before a legitimate court anywhere that English is spoken. The chief justice of England said: "Look you, keeper, you should take off the prisoners' irons when they are at the bar, for they should stand at their ease when they are tried."[5]

Heavy bias prevailed in the courtroom. All 12 objections that the defense raised were overruled. But of the prosecution's 54 objections, only three were overruled.[6] As Eisenschiml notes, "The arrangement of the court was such that the witnesses had their backs toward the defending lawyers and were not permitted by the court to turn their heads to them when under examination. What a handicap this must have been is obvious."[7]

The Best Evidence Goes Missing

One of the trial's most shocking injustices: When John Wilkes Booth was on the run, he kept a diary (also called a memorandum book, it was preprinted for the year 1864). It was recovered from his body after being shot. The diary was turned over to Secretary of War Stanton, who never revealed its existence, except to trusted associates such as Joseph Holt, the trial's Judge Advocate, who also kept silent about it. Even their staunchest defenders can't justify withholding such crucial evidence during the trial. It can legitimately be called "obstruction of justice."

The diary didn't become public knowledge until 1867 when Lafayette Baker (who had a falling out with Stanton) published his book *The History of the Secret Service*. The book made references to the diary, causing a public sensation and an inquiry by the House Judiciary Committee, which found 18 pages of the diary missing. Baker wrote in his book:

> The diary kept by Booth after the murder of the President, to which I referred in connection with the giving of the personal effects of Booth to the Secretary of War, recorded the adventures of the fugitive; one of these was the killing of his horse in the tangled forest to avoid detection, and then sleeping between the animal's legs to get the warmth while it remained in the dead body, during the long hours of the horrible night.[8]

The pages(s) containing this description were missing when Congress received the diary. Also missing was a drawing which Baker said Booth had made of a house. Baker testified that the diary had been intact when he turned it over to Stanton. The War Secretary asserted the pages were already missing, but Baker insisted that Stanton had made no remarks about pages being missing when he received and leafed through it.

Stanton wouldn't have to worry about Baker much longer. He died on July 3, 1868, just 41 years old. His death certificate gave meningitis as cause of death. However, H. Donald Winkler writes in his book *Lincoln and Booth*: "His physician, Dr. William Rickards, testified that his symptoms were typical of arsenic poisoning, but he did not believe Baker had been poisoned 'because no one had the opportunity.'"[9] Controversy has always haunted Baker's death.

Mainstream historians have denounced Baker's claim that pages were removed from the diary after delivery to Stanton because Stanton, Eckert, Holt and Conger all denied it. This is based on the false premise that truth is determined by majority vote. Stanton, Eckert, Holt and Conger were peas in the same pod: Stanton made Eckert his Assistant Secretary of War; appointed Holt to run the conspiracy trial; and awarded Conger $15,000 for his part in finding Booth.

No one would deny that Lafayette Baker was himself a ruthless and corrupt individual. But by saying Baker lied about the missing pages, mainstream historians introduce a contradiction in logic. They forget that without Baker telling the truth about the diary's existence—which Stanton and Holt concealed—we might never have learned there was a Booth diary. The historians then "do a 180"—they claim Baker was honest about the diary existing, but dishonest about pages being missing, while the Stanton group was dishonest about the diary's existence, but honest about no pages being missing!

Judge Holt, who said he kept the diary locked in his safe, attempted to justify his nondisclosure by telling the House Judiciary Committee: "There was nothing in the diary which I could conceive would be testimony against any human being, or for any one except Booth himself, and he being dead, I did not offer it to the Commission."[10]

Even in its mutilated state, Booth's diary clearly revealed that there was no plan to kill until the day of the assassination.

(The full surviving remnant of the diary's text can easily be found online.) The entry for Friday, April 14, said:

> The Ides. Until today nothing was even thought of sacrificing to our country's wrongs. For six months we had worked to capture. But our cause being almost lost, something decisive and great must be done.

If there was no plan to assassinate until April 14—something both Lewis Powell and George Atzerodt independently confirmed—this meant some of the convicted, who had neither been near Washington nor communicated with Booth for some time, such as Samuel Arnold and Dr. Samuel Mudd, couldn't possibly have been guilty of "conspiracy to commit murder."

How could Stanton and Holt have believed Booth's diary was irrelevant to the trial? Why not let the court—including the defense attorneys—decide?

General Benjamin Butler, who had been elected to the U.S. House of Representatives, said:

> Now, what I want to know is this: … If it was good judgment on the part of the gentlemen prosecuting the assassins … to put in evidence the tobacco pipe, spur and compass found in Booth's pocket, why was not the diary, in his own handwriting and found in the same pocket, put in evidence? … I believe that piece of evidence would have shown what the whole case, in my judgment, now shows; that up to a certain hour Booth contemplated capture and abduction, and that he afterward changed his purpose to assassination. … Now what I find fault with in the judge advocate … is

that in his very able and bitter argument against the prisoners, no notice is taken … of this change of purpose and brought to the attention of the men who composed that military tribunal. And if Mrs. Surratt did not know of this change of purpose there is no evidence that she knew in any way of the assassination, and ought not, in my judgment, to have been convicted of taking part in it. … That diary, as now produced, has eighteen pages cut out, the pages prior to the time when Abraham Lincoln was massacred, although the edges as yet show they had all been written over … . Who spoliated that book? Who caused an innocent woman to be hung when he had in his pocket the diary which stated at least what was the idea and purpose of the main conspirator?[11]

While on the run, Booth wrote in his diary: "I have a greater desire and almost a mind to return to Washington and in a measure clear my name, which I feel I can do." Butler said:

How clear himself? By disclosing his accomplices? Who were they? … If we had only the advantage of all the testimony, we might have been able … to find who, indeed, were all the accomplices of Booth; to find who it was who changed Booth's purpose from capture to assassination; who it was that could profit by assassination who could not profit by capture and abduction.[12]

Lincoln historian David M. DeWitt commented in 1909:

So lasting was the sensation caused by this encounter that, when the Congress convened for the July session, the House, on Butler's motion, authorized a special committee to investigate "all the facts and circumstances connected with the assassination tending to show who were the persons engaged in the conspiracy," many of whom, it was declared, "holding high positions of power and authority because of the civil war" acted "through inferior persons who were their tools and instruments."[13]

Stunning revelations came in 1977 when the U.S. Department of the Interior National Park Service requested that the FBI's forensic laboratory examine the diary. (A question had arisen among some scholars as to whether there was "secret writing" in the diary; also, the volume was becoming increasingly difficult to handle due to deterioration from age.) The FBI's report has been largely overlooked, and I am indebted to Don Thomas, not only for calling attention to it, but for clarifying its findings in plain language.

Although the FBI investigation found no "secret writing," it proved that not 18, but 43 sheets (86 pages) had been removed from the original diary. The FBI lab reported:

> 1864 was a leap year and each sheet in the diary contains six dates. Assuming that the first missing sheet was headed January 1, 1864 and the last printed date on the bottom of the last missing sheet was Friday 10, then there would be 162 days, divided by six dates per sheet, accounting for 27 missing sheets or 54 pages. …Twenty-five of the edges of those pages are visible and have been cut. There are two additional sheets (four pages) of which the edges are not observable. …
>
> It was noted that many of the remaining edges of the group of twenty-five missing sheets contain portions of

handwriting which … [if the missing pages were later found] would assist in any future examination relating to these pages.

The sheet (two pages) headed Sunday July 17, 1864 has been torn out. The next missing portion of the diary is the top 1 ½" of the sheet which would be headed Wednesday, August 10, 1864. The side of this sheet representing Saturday August 13 contains some very limited lead markings. The sheets headed August 22 and August 28 have been torn out. The sheet headed December 8 has also been removed.

Between the memoranda sheets following the dated pages and the pages headed "Cash Account – January" there are three additional sheets torn out. There is a cash account sheet for February/March cut out; a cash account sheet for April/May torn out; the top portion of the cash account sheet for May/June removed and the cash account sheet for August/September cut out.

Between the summary of cash account page in the back of the diary and the rear cover there are three torn out sheets, a half torn out sheet and a full torn out sheet, respectively. In total, there are forty-three full sheets (eighty-six pages) missing from the diary.[14]

To clarify, Booth's first entry in what remains of his diary is for April 14, the day of the assassination. Although the diary had preprinted dates, Booth ignored these, as he usually wrote more than the preprinted dates' space allotted. So he hand-wrote his own diary dates. Below we see the entry written "April 14" is on the page preprinted for June 11-13.

What the FBI lab found is that the 27 sheets (54 pages) immediately preceding this page—preprinted January 1 to June 10—had been completely cut from the diary. That these were not blank pages was proven by the fragments of Booth's writing on the remaining stubs (exactly as Congressman Butler had noted 110 years earlier).

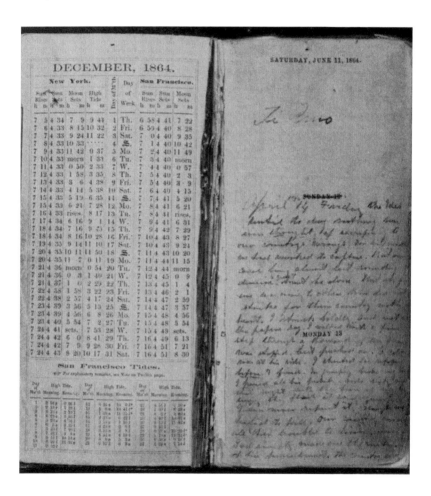

The FBI further found that a portion of the diary had been temporarily detached from the binding; while some pages were permanently removed, others had been glued or "laminated" back in. This especially impacted the critical pages preprinted "June," which included post-assassination details Booth wrote while on the run:

> The diary is glued in place in the middle section. …The four sheets of the diary headed Saturday June 11, Friday June 17, Thursday June 23, and Wednesday June 29 have at an early date been laminated and rebound into the diary.[15]

As Don Thomas points out, for pages to be "rebound" into the diary, they first had to be *unbound*. Apologists for the official story have claimed that Booth himself removed all the missing pages for use as scrap paper or to write letters. Although he *had* torn out two sheets to write a letter to Dr. Richard Stuart, who had provided him and Herold with some food during their escape south, the idea that he needed 43 sheets for such purposes during his 12-day journey has no credibility or evidence to support it. Furthermore, why and how would Booth remove certain pages from his diary and then glue them back in?

The removal and reinsertion of select pages required careful, sophisticated work. Such could be done in the War Department. As Stanton and his immediate aides had kept the diary hidden for two years, who but they would destroy portions of the diary once its existence was revealed, and its surrender demanded by Congress? And why would they engage in such subterfuge unless the diary held content that would incriminate them and/or their associates?

I have only discussed the rudiments of the FBI analysis of Booth's diary. Don Thomas has done much more in-depth reports, which can be found in Chapters 8 and 9 of his book *The Reason Booth Had to Die*, and his articles at https://reason lincoln.com, such as "Congress Investigates Booth's Diary Confession," https://tinyurl.com/43e34fp4.

The Case against Davis Collapses

Secretary Stanton wanted to claim that Booth and his associates murdered Lincoln on orders from Jefferson Davis and the Confederate government, even though the Confederate capital of Richmond had fallen, and Davis and his cabinet were on the run. Defining the murder as an act of war was essential to Stanton's justifying a military instead of civil trial.

At the conspiracy trial's start, a string of false witnesses were procured to testify that Davis and his government had ordered the assassination. Of course, none of these officials were present at the trial to defend themselves or procure counsel. An investigation by the House Judiciary Committee subsequently determined that the evidence against Davis was fabricated, and that the witnesses had been schooled in what to say. For example, the government paid James B. Merritt $6,000 to allege that Davis was behind the murder.[16] His story crumbled under the Judiciary Committee's cross-examination, and he admitted he had lied.

Colonel H. L. Burnett, who had been Assistant Judge Advocate at the conspiracy trial, later conceded: "There was no conclusive evidence to show that Davis sanctioned or approved this undertaking."[17]

Sam Arnold, who had been part of the plan to abduct Lincoln, wrote in his memoirs: "There was never any connection between Booth and the Confederate authorities. I was in Booth's confidence, and had anything existed as such he would have made known the fact to me."[18]

Even U.S. Representative Thaddeus Stevens, one of the leaders of the Radical Republicans, said:

> Those men are no friends of mine. They are public enemies and I would treat the South as a conquered country and settle it politically upon the policy best suited for ourselves. But I know these men, sir. They are gentlemen and incapable of being assassins.[19]

The testimonies against Davis were proven to be perjuries. For a review of these, see Eisenschiml's *Why Was Lincoln Murdered?*, pp. 211-29. If a case could have been made that the Confederacy was actually behind the Lincoln assassination—from which it had nothing to gain and everything to lose—Stanton would not have needed to resort to perjury.

In fact, during the war, Confederate Major Walker Taylor had proposed to Jefferson Davis the possibility of kidnapping Lincoln, but Davis rejected the idea, saying Lincoln might be killed in the process. Davis lived by a Southern code of honor that forbade assassination as a matter of Christian principle. Beyond that, he well knew that Lincoln's death would be disastrous for the South, leaving it at the Radical Republicans' mercy.

Although the case against Davis was bankrupt, Stanton effectively turned his wrath on the small fry: Booth's alleged accomplices.

Notes

1. Samuel Bland Arnold, *Memoirs of a Lincoln Conspirator*, ed. Michael W. Kauffman (Westminster, Maryland: Heritage Books, 2008), 56.
2. Ibid., 59.
3. Martin S. Lederman, "The Law(?) of the Lincoln Assassination," *Columbia Law Review* (March 2017), https://tinyurl.com/4vcfheu4.
4. Otto Eisenschiml, *In the Shadow of Lincoln's Death* (New York: Wilfred Funk, 1940), 144.
5. Otto Eisenschiml, *Why Was Lincoln Murdered?* (1937; reprint, London: Sothis Press, 2023), 241-42.
6. Ibid., 235.
7. Ibid., 236.
8. L. C. Baker, *History of the United States Secret Service* (Philadelphia: L. C. Baker, 1867), 508.
9. H. Donald Winkler, *Lincoln and Booth: More Light on the Conspiracy* (Nashville: Cumberland House, 2003), 296.
10. *Impeachment Investigation* (Washington, D. C.: Government Printing Office, 1868), 285.
11. David M. DeWitt, *Assassination of Abraham Lincoln and Its Expiation* (New York: Macmillan & Co., 1909), 178-79.
12. Ibid., 180.
13. Ibid.

14. "John Wilkes Booth," *FBI Records: The Vault*, Federal Bureau of Investigation, 179–80, https://vault.fbi.gov/ john-wilkes-booth/john-wilkes-booth-part-01-of-01/view.

15. Ibid., 179, 182.

16. Eisenschiml, *Why Was Lincoln Murdered?*, 217.

17. H. L. Burnett, *Assassination of President Lincoln and the Trial of the Assassins*, Ohio Society of New York, 1906, 596, as quoted in Eisenschiml, *Why Was Lincoln Murdered?*, 218.

18. Arnold, 127.

19. Letter of Chief Justice Shea; J. William Jones, ed., *Southern Historical Society Papers*, vol. 1, https://tinyurl. com/43f7ntzd.

CHAPTER 8
WITH JUSTICE FOR NONE

Every person arraigned before the military commission was declared guilty of conspiring to kill the President (except for Ned Spangler, convicted only of helping Booth escape). But as we have seen, this contention had a major fallacy. Up until the day of the assassination—April 14, 1865—Booth's group hadn't planned anything but a kidnapping. Both Lewis Powell (who attempted to kill Secretary of State Seward) and George Atzerodt (who it is dubiously alleged was to assassinate Vice President Johnson) independently reported that Booth did not broach the subject of assassination until the evening of the 14th.

On the morning of the 14th, Booth wrote the following letter to his mother:

Dearest Mother:

I know you expect a letter from me, and am sure you will hardly forgive me. But indeed I have nothing to write about. Everything is dull—that is, has been till last night [the Grand Illumination of D.C., a two-night candle-lit celebration of the Union victory].

Everything was bright and splendid. More so in my eyes if it had been a display in a nobler cause. But so goes the world. Might makes right. I only drop you these few lines to let you know I am well, and to say I have not heard from you. Excuse brevity; am in haste. Had one from Rose.

With best love to you all, I am your affectionate

John[1]

Nothing in this letter indicated that Booth was saying goodbye to his mother, or was about to embark on an epic, life-changing experience. And, again, we read in Booth's diary:

April 14 Friday, The Ides. Until today nothing was even thought of sacrificing to our country's wrongs. For six months we had worked to capture. But our cause being almost lost, something decisive and great must be done.

What transformed Booth from kidnapper in the morning to assassin in the evening? We will examine this, but first let's consider the implications for the convicted.

Dr. Samuel Mudd, as we've noted, treated and made a cast for Booth's broken leg. But Mudd, in Maryland, couldn't have known about Booth's decision in Washington earlier that day to assassinate the President.

Mudd was a Southern sympathizer and had met Booth previously. However, he may not have been lying when he said he didn't recognize Booth on arrival.

Mudd

It was about four in the morning; the house was not well lit; Booth tried to conceal his face with a cloak and left most of the talking to David Herold, who told the doctor his friend had injured himself in a horse fall.

As even military judge Lew Wallace is said to have acknowledged,[2] no one would have even heard Samuel Mudd's name if Booth hadn't broken his leg, an unforeseeable event.

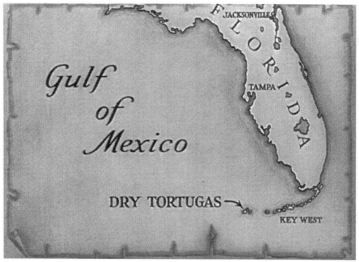

After learning of the assassination, Dr. Mudd reported to authorities the visit from the two strange men. Unfortunate circumstances contributed to his conviction. To treat Booth's fractured leg, he had to cut off his boot. He didn't notice—but a Union officer later did—that Booth's name was inscribed on the boot's interior. He was also shown a picture said to be Booth, and remarked that it was not the man he had treated. However, it wasn't a picture of John Wilkes Booth, but of his brother Edwin Booth. How this error originated is unknown. Were detectives using Edwin Booth's photograph throughout the region?

Dr. Mudd was sentenced to life imprisonment at hard labor at Fort Jefferson on a remote island in the archipelago of Dry Tortugas, Florida, far away from family and reporters. Dry Tortugas is actually west of Key West. This was a continuation of Stanton's "incommunicado" practice that began with hooding suspects soon after they were arrested.

Ironically, Samuel Cox, who had harbored Booth and Herold in a pine thicket for several days, and his half-brother Thomas Jones, who gave Booth and Herold a boat to cross the Potomac, were *not* tried or sentenced, even though they didn't report voluntarily to authorities, as Dr. Mudd had. This was yet another example of the gross discrepancies in justice that haunted the Lincoln case.

There was a deadly outbreak of yellow fever at Dry Tortugas in 1867 which killed many, including the prison's physician. Dr. Mudd took charge, saving numerous lives. President Andrew Johnson, after receiving a petition from the prison's grateful soldiers, pardoned Dr. Mudd. Hollywood made a film about Mudd in 1934, *The Prisoner of Shark Island*, which can be viewed

Arnold and O'Laughlen

on YouTube. It contains both accuracies and inaccuracies, and should not be considered a historical reference.

Samuel Arnold had been a childhood schoolmate of Booth. He was a soldier in the Confederate army, discharged for health reasons in 1864. He was temporarily recruited by Booth in the latter's plot to abduct Lincoln and hold him in exchange for Confederate prisoners. However, after Booth made the rather absurd proposal, in March 1865, of kidnapping Lincoln at Ford's Theatre, and the failed attempt to seize Lincoln's carriage on about March 17, Arnold quit the plot. He did not communicate with Booth after April 1, and was thereafter working at a store at Fort Monroe, Virginia, some 180 miles from Washington.[3] Therefore he couldn't have known of an assassination plot that originated on April 14.

Arnold said of the trial proceedings: "Witnesses were blinded by the amount of glittering gold, as their reward, large sums having been offered for the apprehension of anyone suspected of being connected with the crime. … Let the record of that infamous proceeding stand, in all its branches with its false swearing, subordination of perjury, its hireling witnesses—a towering monument of infamy, commemorating the corruptness and baseness of the hour."[4]

Michael O'Laughlen, another ex-Confederate soldier and Booth childhood friend, was also recruited into the kidnapping plot. But he, like Arnold, dropped out after the March fiascos. O'Laughlen was in Washington at the time of the assassination, but no convincing proof connected him to it. He had gone to the city with friends to view the Illumination (celebration of the Union victory). When O'Laughlen learned that he was wanted for questioning, he turned himself in. His arrest statement is missing from the records. At the trial, several eyewitnesses established that he could not have been anywhere near Edwin Stanton's home at the time the prosecution claimed; nevertheless, he was convicted.

Arnold and O'Laughlen were, like Dr. Mudd, sentenced to life imprisonment at Dry Tortugas, also the destination of Ned Spangler, the hapless Ford's Theatre employee who received a six-year sentence for briefly holding Booth's horse on the night of the assassination.

Ironically, Stanton was not satisfied with sending the four men to Dry Tortugas. A story was fabricated that some scoundrels in New Orleans were going to try to rescue the prisoners. How? Fort Jefferson was not just a prison filled with several hundred armed sentries; it was a formidable military installation.

The design of the fort allows for defense from all sides. At any approach around the fort, 125 cannons can point at a single target. The cannons had a range of about 3 miles and could reload in about a minute. An attacking ship would find themselves with 125 cannon balls a minute raining down upon them. ... The outer walls of the fort are 8 feet thick. This made the fort virtually impenetrable by ship cannon fire since it would take about 50 shots to the same part of the wall to make a hole; from a moving ship with limited cannons, an impossibility. The mere power of the fort served as a deterrent and was never attacked.[5]

The idea that civilians could invade Fort Jefferson by boat, overpower hundreds of armed guards, find and release the Lincon assassination inmates, and sail away, was absurd. Nevertheless, a message dated August 17, 1865, was sent to Colonel H. L. Hamilton, commanding officer at Dry Tortugas:

> The Secretary of War directs that besides taking effectual measures against any attempt to rescue prisoners you will place the four state prisoners—Arnold, Mudd, Spangler and O'Laughlin—under such restraint and within such limits as shall make abortive any attempt at escape or rescue.[6]

As a result, the four prisoners were shackled in solitary confinement in a dark dungeon for several months. O'Laughlen died of yellow fever at the prison in 1867, while Arnold and Spangler were pardoned by Andrew Johnson in 1869, but not before enduring many tortures and deprivations.

Condemned to hang: Powell, Atzerodt

Lewis Powell, a 20-year-old Alabama native, was a Confederate veteran who fought in the battles of Fredericksburg and Gettysburg, being wounded in the latter. He unquestionably tried to assassinate Secretary of State William Seward by stabbing him. He freely admitted it. The only very slightly extenuating circumstance is that he was guilty not of murder, but attempted murder.

The case against **George Atzerodt** is doubtful. As we have noted, he was nobody's idea of a killer; he flatly declined Booth's request to assassinate Vice President Andrew Johnson, and had no motive to do so. Booth even told those Southerners in Virginia who assisted him during his escape that there was never even a plot to murder Johnson. So if Booth did ask Atzerodt, he must have accepted the latter's refusal without pushing the matter.

Atzerodt was just a small-time gofer for Booth, with no deep political convictions, and the conspicuous evidence found in his hotel room had hallmarks of being planted.

David Herold was Booth's riding companion. No evidence exists that he took part in the assassination, though he was an accessory after the fact. While on trial, Herold requested, and

Also destined for the gallows: David Herold

received, permission to write a full confession. He was only permitted to work on it in the courtroom, when he was unhooded and unhandcuffed. He wrote it out fervently over the course of more than one day. However, that confession, like so many other vital documents, simply vanished from the records.[7]

Mary Surratt was perhaps the most tragic trial victim, and her case necessitates much more elaboration than the others. A widow, she ran a boardinghouse in Washington. She was known as kindly and charitable, a devoted mother and devout Catholic. Unquestionably, her son John was a courier for the Confederate Secret Service, but he kept his activities hidden from his mother. John was part of Booth's original plan to abduct Lincoln, and some of the Booth-led meetings took place at the boardinghouse. But John, like Arnold and O'Laughlen, abandoned the scheme when it became unrealistic, and there is no credible evidence that Mary Surratt had attended the meetings. John Surratt was in New York when Lincoln was assassinated.

Fated to hang, and fated to go free: Mary Surratt and her son John

The President was shot at approximately 10:15 PM on April 14, 1865. In less than four hours—even before Booth had been publicly announced as Lincoln's assassin—police descended on the Surratt boardinghouse, seeking Booth and John Surratt. This strongly suggests the government *already* had information about their activity there. While this could have come from several sources, a very likely suspect is Louis Wiechmann (also spelled Weichmann), a "snitch" who lived there as a boarder. Wiechmann had known John Surratt when they were classmates at the seminary of St. Charles College in Maryland (from which neither graduated), and later became John's roommate at the boardinghouse, where, by his own admission, Mary Surratt treated him as a son. But simultaneously he was working in Stanton's War Department, reporting suspicious activities at the Surratt house.

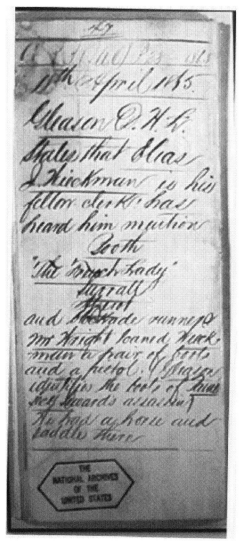

In this rare document found by Don Thomas in the National Archives microfilm, dated April 18, 1865, Captain Daniel H. L. Gleason (Wiechmann's supervisor in the War Department) "states that Louis Wiechmann is his fellow clerk; has heard him mention Booth, 'the French Lady,' Surratt, Atzerodt, and blockade runners." The "French lady" was Sarah Slater, a Confederate courier who could speak French, was well acquainted with Booth and John Surratt, and who visited the Surratt boardinghouse. She may have been a double agent. She was questioned by the War Department after the assassination, but was never tried and mysteriously vanished.[9] She died in Poughkeepsie, New York in 1920.

Weichmann's importance to the Surratt case requires that I briefly discuss him. As Eisenschiml wrote:

Louis J. Wiechmann confided in a fellow clerk, one Captain Gleason, in the office of the commissary general of prisoners, where both of them were employed. Gleason undertook to see that Stanton was informed through Lieutenant Sharp, an assistant provost marshal on the staff of General Augur, while Wiechmann unburdened himself to a United States enrolling officer, named McDavitt, who in turn notified his superiors.[8]

Wiechmann tried to join the Lincoln kidnapping plot. Being a Southernor, it might be argued that his loyalties were shaky and divided—but based on Captain Gleason's account, Wiechmann evidently faked being pro-Confederate to learn more about the kidnapping. As Gleason said in his memoir published in 1911 in *The Magazine of History* (excerpts):

> At the trial of the conspirators Weichman truly said "Major Gleason advised me to talk 'secesh' [secessionist] with those fellows to enlist their sympathy, find out what they were about and, in case they went South go to General C. C. Augur—then Provost Marshal of Washington—get horses for him (Gleason) and myself, so we could go South with them so we could find out just what they were doing; but he (Weichman) replied that that would never do; they were too sharp;" and that I then said the only thing to do was to see Mr. Stanton. ...
>
> My room-mate was Lieutenant Joshua W. Sharp, an Assistant Provost Marshal on General Augur's Staff ... . I called on him and told him Weichman's story. ... I finally convinced him there might be something

in it, and we agreed to notify the authorities. ... Sharp arranged to get word to Secretary Stanton as much as was necessary to secure his assistance ... .[10]

John Surratt said in 1870:

> I proclaim it here and before the world that Louis J. Wiechmann was a party to the plan to abduct President Lincoln. He had been told all about it, and was constantly importuning me to let him become an active member. I refused, for the simple reason that I told him that he could neither ride a horse [hard] nor shoot a pistol, which was a fact. These were two necessary accomplishments for us. My refusal nettled him some ... . I have very little to say of Louis J. Wiechmann. But I do pronounce him a base-born perjurer; a murderer of the meanest hue! Give me a man who can strike his victim dead, but save me from a man who, through perjury, will cause the death of an innocent person.[11]

Major James O'Beirne, the District of Columbia's provost marshal, stated that "Weichman was an accomplice of the conspirators but whose status was subsequently changed."[12]

As in the discredited case against Jefferson Davis, perjury was used against Mary Surratt. Wiechmann was imprisoned under Stanton's orders, but released after agreeing to be a prosecution witness. Edward V. Murphy, who was a court stenographer at the conspiracy trial, had been a high school classmate of Wiechmann, and had often seen him in Washington. He reported:

> While engaged in the work of the War Department one Sunday morning, I had the occasion to visit the room

assigned to Colonel Burnett, who had been summoned to Washington to assist in the prosecution of the alleged conspirators. Seated in the room I observed my old schoolmate, Weichmann, whom I cordially greeted. Upon leaving I was followed into the corridor by Colonel Burnett, who proceeded to question me about Weichmann, my relation with and my knowledge of him. Amazed at the character of the examination, I inquired the reason. Colonel Burnett replied: "You will learn in good time." The following morning in front of the White House I saw Weichmann in manacles being escorted by an armed guard of soldiers to the War Department. The next day I learned that he was charged with being in the conspiracy to murder the President.

I saw nothing more of him until he was placed upon the stand as a witness for the Government during the trial. I observed closely his testimony and the manner in which it was given, and became convinced that he was perjuring himself to save his own neck. When the daily recess for luncheon took place, after Weichmann had been on the stand all morning, he approached me and asked what I thought of his testimony. I replied that I was satisfied that he was falsely swearing away the life of an innocent woman, whom he had repeatedly told me he loved as a mother, in order to save his own worthless carcass, and that I would hold no further communication with him.[13]

After the trial, Wiechmann petitioned Stanton for a govern-ment job, reminding him of the service he had performed for the prosecution. He was duly rewarded with a position in the Philadelphia Customs House.[14]

Eisenschiml relates how Mrs. Surratt came to be hanged:

Louis Wiechmann

> The judge advocate [Joseph Holt], unable to muster the necessary number of votes to hand her over to the hangman, induced the commission to sign her death sentence, with the understanding that a petition for mercy, addressed to the President, would be attached to it. This left the final decision of Mrs. Surratt's fate in the hands of the Chief Magistrate. The guileless officers followed Holt's pleadings, as they had done throughout the trial. But Johnson stated that he had never seen the petition for mercy. When he signed the death warrant on July 5, he did not know that a majority of the court wanted the woman prisoner to live. No one was permitted to see the President until after the execution, and a frantic appeal by one Mr. Brophy, to whom Wiechmann had confessed that he had lied to save his own life, went unheeded.[15]

When the death sentence was read to Mrs. Surratt, she learned she was to be hanged the very next day. Such a short interval was almost unheard of. Stanton was wasting no time in silencing her. As Don Thomas reports:

Senators Preston King and James Henry Lane of Kansas blocked Mary Surratt's daughter, Anna, on the steps of the White House as she desperately tried to reach President Johnson prior to the execution. King and Lane were from the Missouri delegation that previously pressured Lincoln in 1863 to adjust his policies in favor of the Radical agenda … Four months after Mary Surratt was executed Preston King jumped off a ferryboat and drowned, with weights tied around his neck. Four months after that Senator James Lane was said to have committed suicide by shooting himself.[16]

Even Lewis Powell, himself facing the gallows, offered to sign a sworn statement that Mrs. Surratt knew nothing about the plot against Lincoln.

Perhaps Stanton sank to his lowest when he attempted to interfere with Mrs. Surratt's receiving final sacraments from a priest.

An extremely devout woman, Mrs. Surratt fell on her knees and prayed for five minutes when arrested. Even the detectives removed their hats. And when about to walk to the gallows, she told her priest, Father Jacob Walter, "Father, I wish to say something." "What is it?" he asked. "That I am innocent," she said.[17]

Throughout her incarceration, Mrs. Surratt was denied visits from a priest or spiritual counselor. Following her sentence, she had just 24 hours to meet with one. Her priest, Father Walter, planned to administer the final sacraments and requested a pass from the War Department to see her. He received the pass, but made a religious wisecrack to the Irish orderly—namely, that it seemed unlikely that a Catholic woman who went to Communion on Holy Thursday would have been plotting to commit murder the following day, Good Friday.[18] This comment went up the War Department's ranks and set off alarm bells.

General James Hardie then visited Father Walter at his home, and told him the pass he had received was invalid. He had a new pass, signed by Stanton, but would only give it to the priest on one condition. According to Father Walter, Hardie said, "I want you to promise me that you will not say anything about the innocence of Mrs. Surratt." Walter replied, "I cannot let Mrs. Surratt die without the sacraments, so if must say yes, I say yes." And so the pass was given.[19]

But that still wasn't good enough for Stanton. Father Walter related: "Major General Hancock [commander of the District of Columbia] was telegraphed to go and see Archbishop Spalding, so as to prevent me from asserting the innocence of Mrs. Surratt. I received a telegram from the Archbishop's secretary, asking me to keep quiet, and saying that the Archbishop would write me a letter by the evening mail. The letter came. It was no order, but simply a request that I should keep quiet in regard to the innocence of Mrs. Surratt."[20]

The First Amendment to the United States Constitution stipulates that the federal government cannot interfere with freedom of speech or freedom of religion. Secretary Stanton's behavior demonstrated he had no regard for either.

It must be added that the death of those hanged was made as excruciating as possible. Lincoln researcher Robert Arnold, a retired naval surgeon, writes:

> About two hundred spectators "lucky" enough to have passes to the execution had come to be entertained.

Captain Christian Rath did not disappoint them. In addition to providing them with cakes and lemonade, he had made the ropes short enough so that instead of a quick death, the prisoners' agony would be as prolonged as possible. If a condemned person is dropped eight to ten feet, the typical hangman's fracture is produced. A hangman's fracture is a bilateral second cervical vertebrae ring fracture from hyperextension and either distraction or axial compression. Death is almost instantaneous. If the drop is too short, however, the neck is not broken and the victim is slowly suffocated.

Alexander Gardner made photos of the execution, and the pictures that he made of the corpses hanging show that part of Mary Surratt's head is above the scaffold floor, meaning her body only fell about five feet. Additionally, Rath made her noose with only five turns instead of the usual seven, which would make the coils too short to reach the second cervical vertebrae. Those two facts would ensure death by strangulation. Lewis Powell was six feet and two inches tall, and his head is even with the scaffold floor, so he only fell about six feet. The description of his final moments, with "bodily contortions and vibrations of the muscles of the legs," clearly shows that he was not paralyzed. Atzerodt's head is above the scaffold floor, so his drop was about five feet, and his stomach heaved and his legs quivered while suspended. Herold's head is also above the floor, making his drop about five feet as well. He died the hardest, several times trying to draw himself up.[21]

For a clear, chronological, well-documented (about 1,000 endnotes) summary of Mary Surratt's life, substantiating her innocence—including the War Department's use of duress to produce perjured testimony against her—I highly recommend Elizabeth Trindal's *Mary Surratt: An American Tragedy.*

As to **John Surratt**, his case was quite different. Despite having no part in the Lincoln assassination, a $25,000 bounty was placed on him. He fled to Canada, and from there to England.

In England, different people recognized Surratt and contacted Washington, hoping to collect the reward money. They were disappointed. On November 24, 1865, Stanton revoked the reward,[22] and the reason was clear. Stanton was perfectly content to let Surratt stay abroad. If he returned to America, he would receive a civil (jury) trial, rather than facing a military commission; the war had been over too long to justify the latter. Furthermore, the Supreme

Court ruled in 1866 that military commissions trying civilians was unconstitutional when recourse to civil courts was available.[23] And to Stanton, a civil trial could mean unwanted revelations.

Nevertheless, U.S. officials pursued Surratt from England to Italy and finally to Egypt, where he was arrested and then returned to the United States. Surratt's trial, which began on June 10, 1867, was a civil affair; nevertheless, the War Department examined prosecution witnesses before testifying.[24]

The prosecution was reluctant for the trial to start—quite a contrast to the 1865 tribunal, where the prosecution had time to prepare, but defense attorneys, engaged at the last moment, had to scramble to plan their cases. In the Surratt trial, the defense was ready, but the prosecution wasn't—they requested, and received, a continuance. Then, after the jurymen had been assembled, the prosecution objected that they had been improperly assembled on a minor technicality. Another postponement was achieved.[25]

Despite these tactics, and a judge (George P. Fisher) partial to the prosecution, the trial ended in a hung jury, with eight jurors voting "not guilty," four "guilty." Surratt was set free. Undoubtedly some who faced the 1865 military tribunal would have been also, had they received a civil trial.

Notes

1. Don Thomas, *The Reason Lincoln Had to Die* (Chesterfield, Virginia: Pumphouse Publishers, 2013), 68.
2. Otto Eisenschiml, *Why Was Lincoln Murdered?* (1937; reprint, London: Sothis Press, 2023), 469.
3. Confession of Samuel Arnold; William C. Edwards, ed., *The Lincoln Assassination: The Rewards File* (2012), 96,

https://tinyurl.com/2mw93hcr; Letter from Arnold to Dewitt; David M. DeWitt, *Assassination of Abraham Lincoln and Its Expiation* (New York: Macmillan & Co., 1909), 264.

4. Samuel Bland Arnold, *Memoirs of a Lincoln Conspirator*, ed. Michael W. Kauffman (Westminster, Maryland: Heritage Books, 2008), 52-53.

5. "Ft. Jefferson—The Dry Tortugas National Park," *Mark and Cindy's Sailing Blog*, May 21, 2015, https://tinyurl.com/4j8vacr5.

6. Arnold, *Memoirs of a Lincoln Conspirator*, 70.

7. Dave Taylor, "The Confession of David Herold," *LincolnConspirators*, August 27, 2021, https://tinyurl.com/mubmzepc.

8. Eisenschiml, 46.

9. Rebecca Beatrice Brooks, "The Disappearance of Sarah Slater: Confederate Spy and Lincoln Conspirator," *Civil War Saga*, May 14, 2013, https://tinyurl.com/4tc4s3rk.

10. D. H. L. Gleason, "The Conspiracy against Lincoln," *The Magazine of History*, February 1911, 61-62, https://tinyurl.com/233z6r35.

11. "John Surratt's 1870 Account of the Lincoln Assassination Conspiracy" (speech), *University of Missouri—Kansas City School of Law*, https://famous-trials.com/lincoln/2169-surrattspeech.

12. Eisenschiml, 292.

13. Otto Eisenschiml, *In the Shadow of Lincoln's Death* (New York: Wilfred Funk, 1940), 177.

14. Ibid., 177-78.

15. Eisenschiml, *Why Was Lincoln Murdered?*, 294.

16. Thomas, 160.

17. Eisenschiml, *In the Shadow of Lincoln's Death*, 133.

18. Ibid., 134.

19. Ibid., 135.

20. Ibid.

21. Robert Arnold, *The Conspiracy Between John Wilkes Booth and the Union Army to Assassinate Abraham Lincoln* (Louisville, Kentucky: Windsaloft Publishing, 2016), Kindle edition, 355-56.

22. Eisenschiml, *Why Was Lincoln Murdered?*, 202.

23. "Ex parte Milligan," *Wikipedia*, https://en.wikipedia.org/wiki/Ex_parte_Milligan.

24. Eisenschiml, *In the Shadow of Lincoln's Death*, 288-91.

25. Ibid., 271.

CHAPTER 9

EDWIN M. STANTON AND THE NATURE OF EVIDENCE

We now see a consistent line of evidence and "coincidences" pointing to Secretary of War Edwin Stanton:

(1) As reported by Captain Daniel H. L. Gleason, having foreknowledge of the plot to kidnap President Lincoln—but taking no direct actions against the known conspirators prior to the assassination;

(2) On the day of the assassination, under a dishonest pretext, refusal to give Lincoln the protection he requested at Ford's Theatre;

(3) In Congressional testimony, having amnesia about Lincoln's April 14 visit to the War Department, even though other government employees recalled it vividly 40 years later;

(4) Taking charge of a murder case that would have been more properly handled by the Attorney General;

(5) Immediately following Lincoln's assassination, a disruption of telegraph services—then under War Department control;

(6) After telegraph restoration, failure to promptly announce John Wilkes Booth as the assassin;

(7) Deployment of troops in the sequence least likely to apprehend Booth;

(8) Closure of all roads except the one Booth and Herold took;

(9) Failure to chastise Lincoln's bodyguard for deserting his post, while ruthlessly punishing people with little or no connection to the assassination;

(10) Recall of the commanding officer nearest to capturing Booth and Herold, instead sending another detachment commanded by trusted associates;

(11) The execution of Booth by Stanton's select detachment, contrary to official orders;

(12) Cancellation of the court-martial of Boston Corbett (claimed to have shot Booth), precluding investigation of what really happened;

(13) The placement of prisoners in handcuffs, leg irons, and unique canvas hoods, and in complete isolation;

(14) Appointment of a hand-picked military commission to try suspects, rather than a jury trial;

(15) The denial of defense counsel for the accused until approximately the trial's beginning;

(16) Repeated suborning of perjury during the trial;

(17) Concealment of Booth's diary from the commission and public;

(18) Removal of numerous pages from Booth's diary after it was given to Stanton;

(19) Disappearance from War Department files of other documents highly relevant to the assassination, including George Atzerodt's final confession, David Herold's written confession, Michael O'Laughlen's arrest statement, Lieutenant Baker's official report after bringing Booth's body to Washington, and more;

(20) Denial of religious sacraments to Mary Surratt, conditional on the priest's silence concerning her innocence;

(21) The sending of the four convicted prisoners who were not hanged to Dry Tortugas, perhaps the most remote prison imaginable;

(22) Placing the four in solitary confinement at Dry Tortugas for months, on the absurd pretext that rescuers might invade the impregnable fortress;

(23) Withdrawal of the reward for John Surratt in apparent hopes of keeping him in Europe;

(24) The War Department's screening of witnesses in the Surratt trial, even though it was a civil undertaking;

(25) Last but not least: motive. Lincoln and Seward—the only actual victims of assassination attempts—were the only prominent officials obstructing the Reconstruction plan formulated by Stanton and the Radical Republicans.

19th century ivory plaque (scrimshaw) seen in an auction catalogue.
Belief that Stanton was behind the assassination isn't new.
As the convicted prisoners were hanged on July 7, 1865, the July
22 date may possibly be when the scrimshaw was completed.

In 1937, Otto Eisenschiml acknowledged that the evidence against Stanton—while cumulatively overwhelming—remained circumstantial unless connections could be drawn between Stanton and Booth.

Because the proof concerning Stanton *was* circumstantial, mainstream historians today ridicule Eisenschiml, ignoring the depth and quality of his research. Today, Edward Steers is possibly the most mainstream of mainstream Lincoln assassination historians. Before saying anything critical of him, let me acknowledge the service that he and his coeditor William Edwards provided the public by digitizing innumerable transcripts of handwritten documents found in the National Archives pertaining to the assassination, in their volume *The Lincoln Assassination: The Evidence* (although according to Don Thomas, who has extensively studied the archive documents on microfilm, pertinent material remains missing in that book).

That said, in the "Edwin McMasters Stanton" entry of his *Lincoln Assassination Encyclopedia*, Steers gushes that Stanton "stepped into the breach at a moment of national crisis and brought a steadying influence," and "Stanton became a target for all of the bizarre conspiracy theories, beginning with Otto Eisenschiml in 1937 and continuing right up to the present."[1] Elsewhere in the tome, Steers says Eisenschiml "manipulated the data" and refers to "Eisenschiml's ridiculous theory."[2] Evidently Steers hopes that pejoratives like "bizarre" and "ridiculous" will dissuade people from actually reading Eisenschiml's books and making up their own minds.

He sneers at Eisenschiml as "a professionally trained chemist turned avocational historian." Yet according to his *Wikipedia* biography, Steers himself earned his college degrees in microbiology (1959) and molecular biology (1963), was an adjunct professor of biochemistry from 1966 to 1986, and did not begin writing on history until 1994. His bio mentions no degrees earned in history.[3]

Many people competently wear more than one hat during their lifetimes. Abraham Lincoln was popularized as having been a rail-splitter during his youth; this doesn't mean he had to stay a rail-splitter for life.

Steers says, "Eisenschiml's case against Stanton has been thoroughly refuted, principally by the research of James O. Hall and William Hanchett."[4]

As Steers gives the impression that Hanchett took Eisenschiml behind the woodshed and gave him a beating, I decided to buy a copy of Hanchett's book *The Lincoln Murder Conspiracies*; I read his chapter "Otto Eisenschiml's Grand Conspiracy." I found Hanchett using the same ad hominem tactics as Steers. He says "Eisenschiml was glad to give up his career in chemistry, for he craved the recognition not received by members of the profession."[5] Later he says: "Possibly his judgement was warped by the excitement of discovering long-neglected documents and by the expectation of winning as an historian the recognition he had failed to receive as a chemist."[6] Thus Hanchett asserts that Eisenschiml's motive was not seeking truth, just personal fame. But the same claim could be made about Hanchett, Steers, or any author.

Later he says, "Eisenschiml's falsifications and perversions, camouflaged by the man's constant protestations of scientific objectivity, have thus erected a formidable barrier against an understanding of Lincoln's assassination."[7]

To the contrary, Eisenschiml wrote two books about the Lincoln assassination, *Why Was Lincoln Murdered?* and *In the Shadow of Lincoln's Death*. I have read both books, and do not recall Eisenschiml ever discussing himself or boasting of his own objectivity. These "constant protestations" Hanchett refers to may exist elsewhere, but certainly not in Eisenschiml's Lincoln assassination books.

And how about Hanchett's analysis of Eisenschiml's work?

■ One of the most powerful points Eisenschiml made concerned Booth's diary—which Stanton and Judge Advocate Holt kept hidden for two years, and, when finally turned over to Congress, had many pages missing. After his 1963 death, Eisenschiml was vindicated regarding this matter by the FBI's forensic lab analysis, which found that 43 sheets (86 pages) had been removed.

What does Hanchett say about this? Nothing. His chapter on Eisenschiml doesn't refer to the diary, even once. After all, it's pretty hard to justify flagrant obstruction of justice. (Hanchett does mention the diary elsewhere in his book, when discussing other conspiracy writers.)

- What about Eisenschiml's condemnation of Lincoln's body-guard, John Parker, deserting his post? How does Hanchett refute this? He writes: "James O. Hall has suggested 'that the President [had] dismissed him and told him to take a seat and enjoy the play. This would have been in character for Lincoln.'"[8] In other words, Hanchett's "refutation" is just speculation unsupported by any factual evidence.

- What about Eisenschiml pointing out that no soldiers at Garrett's farm corroborated Boston Corbett shooting Booth? How does Hanchett debunk this? He says: "It is also significant that none ever said he could not have shot him."[9] That's not refutation; it's playing tit for tat.

- As to the extraordinary conditions the accused prisoners were subjected to, Hanchett writes: "Nor is there the slightest sub-stance to Eisenschiml's argument that the hoods, executions, and the treatment of the prisoners at Dry Tortugas were all calculated to keep Booth's friends from talking. …[All] were represented by counsel. It is absurd to state they had no opportunity to talk."[10]

But there's a lot Hanchett omits: He forgets to mention that "counsel" wasn't provided, for the most part, until the trial began;

that defense attorneys were not allowed to consult with their clients privately (I have found a single exception to this); that the guards were forbidden to speak to the prisoners and vice versa; and that the canvas hoods (which Hanchett cannot justify) made communication virtually impossible anyway. Hanchett provides no explanation for why the prisoners not hanged were all sent to the remote prison at Dry Tortugas, where for months they were shackled in solitary confinement—hardly conducive to "talking."

I find it abhorrent that Hanchett says nothing against the barbaric treatment of the prisoners.

Hanchett is correct when he points out that the three convicted men who survived—Mudd, Arnold, and Spangler—did not implicate Stanton after their release. But Stanton had no way of knowing just how much each man knew, and clearly wasn't taking chances.

This isn't to say Hanchett never makes a valid observation. He challenges Eisenschiml's criticism of Stanton's failure to close Booth and Herold's escape road by pointing out that there were no telegraph stations and limited troops near that road. However, Eisenschiml *already* acknowledged that.[11] Given the speed with which Stanton organized and sent the Conger detachment, why couldn't troops with telegraph facilities have been dispatched to that road? Booth was, after all, following the same route long planned for Lincoln's abduction, a scheme the federal government already knew about.

I had been led to believe that Hanchett gave Eisenschiml a beating behind the woodshed. Instead, it was Hanchett who took the beating—and by a man no longer even living to defend himself. Perhaps we should replace the phrase "hatchet job" with "Hanchett job."

Above, I pointed out 25 pieces of circumstantial evidence against Edwin Stanton. Coincidences do happen. But any good police detective will tell you that *too many* coincidences normally constitute a preponderance of evidence pointing to guilt.

District attorneys regularly make such correlations of circumstantial evidence to prove criminal cases. Let's say a man murders his wife to collect insurance money. It's highly unlikely he would do this while being videotaped, or right before witnesses. So the prosecutor must accumulate *indirect* evidence of guilt. For example, he might show the jury that the accused owned the murder weapon, or that his fingerprints were on it, that the victim's blood was on his clothing, that he was observed leaving the crime scene, that he had motive, etc. Are America's district attorneys *paranoid* to do this? Are they fabricating "bizarre," "ridiculous" conspiracy theories? No; it's essential, and very normal, in prosecuting crimes. A preponderance of evidence demonstrates highly probable criminal intent.

Interestingly, in his encyclopedia, Edward Steers says of Jefferson Davis: "While there is no direct evidence linking Davis to Lincoln's death, there are several smoking guns that point in his direction."[12]

So, Steers *is* willing to accept indirect evidence as "smoking guns" of guilt—just so long as they point to Jefferson Davis (whom he doesn't definitely accuse) and not to Edwin Stanton.

In the famous Alfred Hitchcock movie *Rear Window*, L. B. Jeffries, played by James Stewart, becomes frustrated by the skepticism of his detective friend Tom Doyle, despite all the circumstantial evidence Jeffries has provided that a neighbor has murdered his wife. Finally he says in exasperation, "Well, then what do you need as probable cause for a search warrant? Bloody footprints leading up to his front door?"

This is what Steers and other mainstream historians demand: bloody footprints on Stanton's doorstep. Nothing less than a signed, notarized confession by the War Secretary is deemed worthy of consideration. Nothing less than a Matthew Brady photograph of Stanton handing Booth the derringer as he entered the Presidential box.

I have been a journalist since 1986, when I published my first articles for *The New American* magazine. Over the decades, I have found that the status quo for most major historical events is that an *official story* is given to the public, while a *back story*, the true story, is kept concealed. And that largely happens because, as finance journalist Ferdinand Lundberg documented in his 1937 book *America's Sixty Families*, America is run—behind the façade of "democracy"—by a wealthy oligarchy that keeps its thumb on both politicians and the press. One place to start researching this is my book *Thirteen Pieces of the Jigsaw*, which has chapters bringing out the back stories of the Spanish-American War, the sinking of the *Lusitania*, the attack on Pearl Harbor, the atomic bombings of Japan, the Korean War, and other major events. For a comprehensive discussion of the oligarchy's manipulations, from the Panic of 1907 right up to Climate Change restrictions, I suggest watching my 2023 public PowerPoint presentation *An Oligarchy Controls America* on the Rumble channel at https://tinyurl.com/4aphhbck.

The Lincoln assassination is really no different. There was an official story and a back story. Mainstream historians like Steers simply regurgitate the official propaganda that has been sold to the public since the beginning. Thus they do almost nothing to advance our understanding of the event, while the real investigative detectives, like Eisenschiml and Thomas, are scoffed at as "conspiracy theorists."

For those who believe the views this book expresses are outlandish, I invite them to watch the documentary *They've Killed President Lincoln*, which aired on NBC on February 12, 1971 (Lincoln's birthday). Narrated by Hollywood actor Richard Basehart, and produced by David L. Wolper Productions (*North & South*, *Roots*, *Four Days in November*, and more than 200 other features), it asked many of the same questions posed by this book and Eisenschiml: Why did Stanton lie to Lincoln when the President asked for Major Eckert to be his bodyguard? Why did the assigned bodyguard desert his post? Why did the telegraph service shut down just after the assassination? Why was Booth's escape route left unpatrolled? Why did Stanton suppress the existence of Booth's diary and remove pages from it? Why did key reports disappear from War Department files? The documentary pointed a clear finger at Edwin Stanton. As this book goes to press, you can watch it at https://www.youtube.com/watch?v=oQHSBY7naMY (https://tinyurl.com/yc2c8w65).

That the documentary was featured on network television proves that, 50 years ago, this book's concepts were acceptable within the mainstream, and were *not* considered "bizarre" and "ridiculous" as Steers now puts it. That was also demonstrated 87 years ago, when Eisenschiml's book became a Book-of-the-Month Club selection.

Today, history is under attack as never before. The melting down of Robert E. Lee's statue and the outlawing of Confederate flags are designed to erase history. Likewise, the arrival of historians like Steers and Hanchett did not enhance history, but suppressed it, stifling logical inquiry

The case against Stanton is now stronger than ever, but remains circumstantial, as he so well used his autocratic power to bury the evidence trail. This, I regret, forces me to resort to a certain amount of speculation in the next chapter. However, Don Thomas has drawn us closer to meaningful connections, utilizing documents that were unavailable to Eisenschiml. Let's take a look.

Notes

1. Edward Steers, *The Lincoln Assassination Encyclopedia* (New York: HarperCollins, 2010), Kindle edition, 502, 503.
2. Ibid., 279.
3. "Edward Steers Jr.," *Wikipedia,* https://en.wikipedia.org/wiki/Edward_Steers_Jr.
4. Steers, *Lincoln Assassination Encyclopedia*, 198.
5. William Hanchett, *The Lincoln Murder Conspiracies* (Urbana: University of Illinois Press, 1983), 160.
6. Ibid., 181.
7. Ibid., 209.
8. Ibid., 173.
9. Ibid., 178.
10. Ibid., 179-80.
11. Otto Eisenschiml, *Why Was Lincoln Murdered?* (1937; reprint, London: Sothis Press, 2023), 102.
12. Steers, *Lincoln Assassination Encyclopedia*, 149.

CHAPTER 10
BOOTH AND A WIDER CONSPIRACY

Why were prisoners hooded, denied the ability to communicate, and then, by a kangaroo court, either hanged or sentenced to imprisonment on a desolate island? Why was Booth's diary concealed for two years, then many of its pages destroyed when subpoenaed by Congress? What was Stanton so desperately trying to hide? *It could only be evidence that would incriminate himself, the War Department, and/or the Radical Republicans they represented.*

To achieve their postwar goal of a brutal Reconstruction, Stanton and the Radical Republicans needed Lincoln dead. While this could have been accomplished by something as simple as poisoning the President, a poisoning would be nearly impossible to blame on the Confederacy. Something dramatic was needed: an assassination. But that required an assassin. Stanton needed a patsy, someone with ties to the South who could be prodded into killing Lincoln.

John Wilkes Booth was known to be adamantly pro-Confederate. Through snitches like Louis Wiechmann, the War Department was aware of Booth's plans to abduct the President.

Furthermore, Booth, on a number of occasions, had intimated his willingness to kill. For example, John Surratt, one of Booth's cohorts in the kidnapping plot, related:

> At this meeting I explained the construction of the gates [at a Washington bridge], etc., and stated I was confident the government had wind of our movement, and the best thing we could do would be to throw up the whole project. Everyone seemed to coincide in my opinion, except Booth, who sat silent and abstracted. Arising at last and bringing his fist upon the table he said, "Well, gentlemen, if the worst comes to the worst, I shall know what to do."

> Some hard words and even threats then passed between him and some of the party. Four of us then arose, one saying, "If I understand you to intimate anything more than the capture of Mr. Lincoln I for one will bid you goodbye." Everyone expressed the same opinion. We all arose and commenced putting our hats on. Booth perceiving probably that he had gone too far, asked pardon saying that he "had drank too much champagne."[1]

Stanton knew Booth was a firecracker waiting for his fuse to be lit. With his connections to Southerners in the abduction plan (Surratt, Powell, Arnold, O'Laughlen, Atzerodt), he was the perfect tool to carry out the assassination, which could then be blamed on the Confederacy. This required motivating Booth and facilitating the murder. That in turn necessitated infiltrating federal agents into Booth's circle without his knowing it. After the murder, all evidence of these agents would be stricken from the record, while any links to the South would be played up and even fabricated.

We previously noted the humdrum letter Booth wrote to his mother on the morning of April 14. Nothing yet indicated that he was planning to turn assassin later that day.

Mainstream historians say what prompted Booth to kill was his learning that Lincoln would be at Ford's Theatre. But if this was simply an idea in Booth's head, how did Stanton and Eckert know about it? We've seen their dishonesty in denying Lincoln the protection he sought, which indicates foreknowledge of what would occur later. Where did the information come from? Certainly not from Booth's convicted accomplices, Powell and Atzerodt. They knew nothing of the murder plot until 7:30 to 8 that evening.

Whoever reported it to the War Department may have also provided Booth with his *inside information*, increasing the appeal of assassination:

Inside Information

We've commented on Booth's confidence that he would only need a single-shot derringer to dispose of the President, implying advance knowledge that Lincoln would be unprotected.

It may not be happenstance that Lincoln's bodyguard, John F. Parker, deserted his post shortly before the assassination. While hapless employees of Ford's Theatre were arrested and interrogated after the assassination, Parker went completely unpunished. History has virtually erased his name. Edwards and Steers' *The Lincoln Assassination: The Evidence*, the 1,400-page compendium of government files concerning the assassination, refers to Parker only once—in a footnote. During the 1865 trial of the alleged conspirators, he was never called to testify, or even mentioned.

As we've noted, Parker showed up for duty three hours late on the 14th. What caused this delay? Was it from habitual slackness, or because he was being instructed to leave his post? If the latter, Parker must have protested and argued, but then finally been persuaded by assurances of immunity, and perhaps threats if he failed to obey.

But Booth had more inside information than absence of a bodyguard. Booth later told his riding companion David Herold that, before assassinating the President, he had "fastened the door" behind him to prevent others from entering.[2]

The badly wounded Major Rathbone testified:

> On reaching the outer door of the passage-way, I found it barred by a heavy piece of plank, one end of which was secured in the wall, and the other resting against the door. It had been so securely fastened, that it required considerable force to remove it. This wedge or bar was about four feet from the door. Persons upon the outside were beating against the door for the purpose of entering. I removed the bar, and the door was opened.[3]

The day after the assassination, Abram Olin, justice of the Supreme Court of the District of Columbia, examined the Presidential box, accompanied by Clara Harris, Major Rathbone's fiancée. He reported:

> My attention was called to the incision into the wall that was prepared to receive the brace that fitted into the corner of the panel of the outer door ... The indentation

upon the panel of the door where the brace might have been fixed from against the wall, was quite perceptible, and the brace was so fixed that it would be very difficult to remove it from the outside. I think it could not have been done without breaking the door down.[4]

Also, the *inner* door, leading immediately to the President's box, had a peephole carved into it, enabling the assassin to view his target before entering. Judge Olin related:

I procured a light and examined very carefully the hole through the door. ... It was a freshly-cut hole, the wood apparently being as fresh as would have been the instant it was cut.[5]

Booth had neither the skill nor time to prepare the two doors in this precise manner. The plank (later sometimes called part of a music stand) necessitated an incision in the wall plaster, a perfect fit at a perfect length from the door. This would have also required re-covering the incision with the wallpaper, and cleaning up the plaster fragments off the floor. Mainstream historians have claimed Booth did this, and also created the peephole in the door to the Presidential box by carving through it with a penknife; he then would have had to clean up the wood shavings. How could the famous actor have performed all this time-consuming, skilled, and noisy carpentry work without being heard and spotted by the Ford's Theatre staff, thus arousing suspicion and ruining his assassination plans?

Another of the April 14, 1865 mysteries is how accomplice Lewis Powell gained entry to Secretary of State William Seward's home. Powell rang the doorbell, displayed a small package, and told the servant he had brought medication prescribed by Seward's physician, Dr. Verdi. Despite no help from the servant (who was suspicious of Powell), he knew where Seward was located—in a third floor bedroom—and knew exactly where the staircase was. Information concerning the physician and house layout could only have come from inside. How did Powell know?

The answer may be in the long-lost confession of George Atzerodt, who was hanged for allegedly planning to assassinate Vice President Andrew Johnson. After having his hood removed, and being given false hopes that he might be allowed to live, Atzerodt made his final confession to Provost Marshal James McPhail. It was done without duress, and recorded by detective John L. Smith, who worked for McPhail, but was also Atzerodt's brother-in-law. The confession was disallowed during the military tribunal; it then—like other key documents—vanished from War Department files. It was presumed lost for over a century. But in 1977 a copy was found in the files of W. E. Doster, who had been Atzerodt's attorney, by one of Doster's descendants. It can be read, with annotations, at www.reasonlincoln.com; click "articles." (See also https://tinyurl.com/5eajjdvx.)

Was Atzerodt hanged, and his confession destroyed, because he mentioned federal agents who had penetrated Booth's conspiracy? If these agents were revealed in court, it could have lit a trail of gunpowder leading back to Stanton and the War Department.

The confession has been criticized as being rambling, jumping from topic to topic. This is because Atzerodt was being asked questions. The confession only records the answers, not the questions, resulting in its disjointed appearance. When discussing Booth's accomplices, Atzerodt said:

James Donaldson … only saw him one time and this was Wednesday [April 12] previous to the murder. He was having an interview with Booth and told him to meet him on Friday evening and he replied he would and left and went up Penn. Avenue towards the Treasury Building. I was under the impression he came on with Booth.

Secretary Seward employed a messenger/aide named James Donaldson. The latter was supposed to be attending Seward on the evening of April 14, but traded shifts with George Robinson,[6] who wound up getting stabbed trying to protect Seward from his assailant. Donaldson returned to the Seward home a few minutes after the attacks on Lincoln and Seward, which had been synchronized.

It's quite a coincidence that James Donaldson requested the evening of the assassination off, at the very time Booth had planned to meet a man named James Donaldson. The Treasury Building, which Atzerodt said he last saw Donaldson heading toward on Pennsylvania Avenue, was adjacent to the State Department—and directly across the street from Seward's home.

Atzerodt described Donaldson as "a low chunky man," which fits his picture (following page). However, a major discrepancy is that Atzerodt also recalled him as "23 or 24 years of age," whereas Seward's aide was in his forties. Inasmuch as Atzerodt claimed he only saw him once, apparently on the street with his hat on, possibly at night, he might have erred about the age.

While acknowledging this contradiction, we may still ask: Are we discussing two different James Donaldsons, or the same man? Seward's aide could certainly have told Booth everything he needed for Powell to gain access to the Secretary's home.

Why didn't the government investigate Booth's accomplice named James Donaldson?

Booth had yet another means of learning about the Seward home. Atzerodt also said:

> I overheard Booth when in conversation with Wood [alias of Powell] say, that he visited a chambermaid at Seward's House and that she was pretty. He said he had a great mind to give her his diamond pin.[7]

Some believe the woman referred to was Margaret Coleman. The Seward family maintains a digital archive. It says about Margaret Coleman:

> Household servant of the Seward Family in Washington, D.C. during the 1865 assassination attempt on William H. Seward. Supposedly also nursed Fanny Seward [William's daughter] during her illness and was with her

at her [untimely] death. Later in life, served in Charles Sumner's home until his death.[8]

So, aside from James Donaldson, Booth might have received inside information from Margaret Coleman. What is striking about the above passage is that she later worked for Charles Sumner. *Wikipedia* notes: "During the war, Sumner led the Radical Republican faction, which was critical of President Abraham Lincoln for being too moderate toward the South."[9]

Whether it was Donaldson, Coleman, or another servant, the military commission never identified Booth's "insider" at the Secretary's home.

One more circumstance that may suggest Booth had inside information is the ease with which he exited Washington via the Navy Yard Bridge leading south into Maryland. Bridges leading to and from Washington were patrolled by federal troops, under these orders: "No person excepting General Officers will be passed over any of the several crossings between the hours of 9:00 P.M. and daylight without the countersign and a pass."[10] This order had been in effect since January 1863—well over two years. Booth, who spent much time in Washington, presumably knew about this curfew. Sergeant Silas Cobb, in charge of the Navy Yard Bridge, questioned Booth, who arrived about 10:25 (10 minutes after the assassination), brazenly gave his name as Booth, and claimed he didn't know about the rule, but needed to get to his home in Maryland. Cobb let him pass. A few minutes later, Herold arrived. He gave his name as "Smith," said he was out late due to a tryst with a lady, didn't know about the rule, but needed to get home. Cobb let him pass also.

It might be rationalized that Cobb was simply good-natured and that, with the war effectively over, decided to be lax about following the curfew order. However, Booth and Herold were taking quite a chance by believing they could both smooth-talk their way past the guards. If refused, they would have been trapped in Washington, and very likely ensnared by the frantic manhunt, Booth having already been identified as the President's assassin. For letting the duo escape, in violation of standing orders, Sergeant Cobb suffered no punishment at the hands of the normally ruthless Stanton. It does raise the question if, as in other cases, the "fix was in" at the bridge.

The Missing Letter to the *Intelligencer*

When questioned by Special Judge Advocate John Bingham, David Herold, Booth's riding companion, said Booth told him that he had 35 accomplices in the Lincoln assassination.[11] While this may have been hyperbole, Seward assailant Lewis Powell, when asked about Booth's accomplices by Thomas Eckert, said, "All I can say about that is, you have not got the one-half of them."[12] And we've seen that Booth did receive special assistance and inside information. Herold also stated:

> He [Booth] said five men ought to have met him [in the South]. ... He said that there was a letter he wrote, and they all signed their names to it, I mean the five, giving their reasons for doing such and such things. He told me this the day before we crossed into Virginia. He said it would be published. ... He said it would be in the *Intelligencer* [a Washington newspaper].[13]

While Booth and Herold were staying in a pine thicket near the home of Southern sympathizer Samuel Cox, Cox and his step-brother Thomas Jones brought them food and newspapers every day. Booth looked in vain for news of his letter being published.

John Mathews

The letter didn't appear in the *Intelligencer*, but the newspaper's editor, John F. Coyle, was interrogated. Coyle said he knew nothing about it. The interrogation eventually brought a new figure out of the woodwork: actor John Mathews, a friendly acquaintance of Booth who had appeared in *Our American Cousin* on the night of the assassination.

Mathews told a rather strange story. He said that on the day of the assassination, around 4PM, Booth was riding along on his horse, and spotted Mathews on the street. He handed Mathews a sealed envelope and asked if he would deliver it to the *Intelligencer* the next day.

After the assassination, Mathews said, he went from Ford's Theatre to his rented room, badly shaken. Suddenly he remembered the envelope Booth had given him. He tore it open. Inside was a letter, in which Booth listed what he considered noble reasons for killing the President. Mathews said it was signed by Booth, and, in Booth's handwriting, the names of Payne (Powell), Atzerodt, and Herold. Mathews said he was afraid of being incriminated by having the letter, so he burned it.[14]

But Mathews' story has lots of weaknesses:

- Surely when Booth wrote the letter, he already had a plan for getting it to the *Intelligencer*. Randomly spotting Mathews on the street seems "a likely story."

- None of Booth's convicted confederates knew of a plan for murder until nearly 8PM on the 14th—why, at 4PM, was Booth already so sure they would agree to it that he would sign their names?

- Why, without their permission, would he publicly announce his accomplices, which would ensure their arrest and prosecution?

- What if Mathews had gotten suspicious, and read the letter *before* the assassination? Booth's entire scheme could have gone up in smoke, with the President alive, and Booth and his accomplices arrested. Would Booth take such a chance?

- Booth knew that Mathews was performing in *Our American Cousin* that evening, and that Mathews would therefore be among the first witnesses to the assassination. Could he really believe that, after seeing Booth kill the President, Mathews would still deliver the letter to the *Intelligencer* the next day, no questions asked?

- Booth told Herold that five *other* men signed the letter. If Booth signed Herold's name (as Mathews claimed), why didn't he simply tell Herold, "By the way, David, I signed your name"? Because if Mathews' story is correct, Herold would have seen his own name in the *Intelligencer* anyway once the letter was published.

Clearly, Mathews' story is suspicious. It had no corroboration—no one saw Booth give him the envelope, or saw the letter, or saw him burn it. As to the supposed signatures in Booth's handwriting, it appears that Mathews simply regurgitated the names of the three men the military commission had hanged. Since neither they nor Booth were alive, they couldn't contradict Mathews' claim.

But this wasn't the only suspect thing about John Mathews. When Booth was planning the original kidnapping, he had guns stored at a Maryland tavern. After the assassination, he picked up these guns during his run south. Booth originally had the weapons shipped from New York in his wardrobe box. Detectives found that box in Mathews' home. Mathews claimed Booth simply gave it to him as a gift.[15]

In the War Department archives is a letter addressed to Edwin Stanton from R. W. Walker of Boston, written a week after the assassination. Walker warned, "It is thought Mathews of Ford's Theatre is knowing to all of Booth's proceedings."[16] (Booth had been in Boston just eight days before the assassination.)[17]

Then there was Mathews' relationship with William P. Wood, whom Stanton appointed warden of Washington's Old Capitol Prison, which housed thousands of inmates, including political prisoners and Confederate POWs. As Don Thomas notes:

> But Stanton's most professional source of Confederate secrets came from William P. Wood, the warden of the Old Capitol Prison. … Wood had some 30 agents and spies under his authority, and many agents, such as James Hall, intercepted mail deliveries between Richmond and Washington and brought the letters to Wood at the prison. Wood skillfully opened the letters, then read and copied the ones that had secret messages, sending the copies directly to Stanton.[18]

Subsequently Stanton made Wood his intelligence chief as head of the Secret Service.

When an attempt was made to impeach President Andrew Johnson in 1867, the House of Representatives Judiciary Committee conducted an extensive hearing. One witness called to testify was John T. Ford, owner of Ford's Theatre. He had been imprisoned at the Old Capitol Prison after the assassination. John Mathews visited him there. In his testimony, Ford said: "Mathews knew Wood very well. He came to visit me in prison, when I found that Wood and he were old friends. Mathews was never a prisoner there to my knowledge."[19]

How is it that the young actor Mathews, self-described as a "comedian," a friend of Booth, was also good friends with Stanton's intelligence chief Wood? This meant Mathews was only one step removed from Stanton.

What really went on with Mathews and the *Intelligencer* letter? Here is an exchange that occurred during Wood's own testimony at the impeachment hearing:

> Q. Was not the letter to be published in the Intelligencer?
>
> A. I understood it was intended for publication in the Intelligencer.
>
> Q. Do you know whether it was ever presented to the Intelligencer?
>
> A. I am sure that if ever any such letter was written it was never presented to the parties in the Intelligencer office. It never went further than the Old Capitol.
>
> Q. Was it in the Old Capitol?

A. I think it was brought there by this man Mathews.[20]

Wood had just slipped up, flatly contradicting his friend Mathews' claim of destroying the letter. Wood had admitted that Mathews brought the letter to the Old Capitol Prison, where Wood, as warden, opened letters and relayed anything of interest to Stanton.

Stunned, the Congressmen on the Judiciary Committee wanted to know more:

Q. Do you pretend to say now that you do know all about this letter?
A. I do not think I used that expression. I only mean to say that I know such a letter was written.
Q. And yet you have never seen it?
A: I have never seen it.[21]

Wood also prevaricated by saying Mathews brought the letter in as a prisoner, but that the guards bungled the job of searching him:

Q. Then he must have had it on his person when he was brought there as a prisoner?
A. If it was on his person in the Old Capitol, it went in with him as a prisoner.
Q: Did you search his person?
A. It was the rule to search all prisoners, and I am confident that he was searched when he went in; but it was an easy thing to secrete it.[22]

All this made no sense. If Wood never saw the letter, and his guards never found it, how could he know Mathews brought it to the Old Capitol? And why would Mathews bring a highly incriminating letter into prison, in the improbable hope that he could "secrete" it when the guards searched him?

What would make more sense is that Mathews brought the letter to his "old friend" Wood as an informant.

The Whistle

At the trial of the alleged Lincoln conspirators, the following items found on Booth were placed in evidence: a knife, pair of pistols, belt, holster, file, pocket compass, spur, tobacco pipe, carbine, cartridges, and bills of exchange.[23] However, Booth's diary was withheld, and so was ... his whistle (picture from the Ford Theatre National Historic Site).

Why was Booth carrying a whistle? The answer was pretty clearly revealed by Colonel John A. Foster, one of the War Department's assassination investigators, within his very detailed report of April 23, 1865:

> A horseman was seen riding rapidly up 10th Street past Massachusetts Avenue shortly after the murder in a northerly direction. About the time or immediately prior to his passing, a shrill whistle was thrice repeated, was heard up 10th Street, an answering whistle on 9th Street and one on Massachusetts Avenue between 9th and 10th apparently in reply to them.[24]

In the Steers and Edwards' *Evidence* book, transcripts of several witness statements concerning these coordinated whistles can be read.[25] Some of the witnesses also recalled that, simultaneously, a man leapt on a horse that was tied at a vacant lot near Ford's Theatre, and took off. This couldn't have been Booth, whose horse was held for him by Joseph Burroughs, directly behind the theater.

Why would Booth carry a whistle? A fairly reasonable guess: to signal accomplices that "the deed is done." The whistle's "shrill" sound could be heard and distinguished above the frantic shouts following the assassination.

But who was blowing the "answering" whistles on 9th Street, 10th Street and Massachusetts Avenue, and why? A mainstream explanation might be that they were acknowledging that other assassination attempts would now be set in motion. But an answering whistle could not have come from Powell (Seward's attempted assassin), who wasn't in that district, and was unlikely to thus call attention to himself before entering Seward's home. Nor could it have come from any elusive would-be assassin of Stanton, who didn't live near there either. Nor from Atzerodt, who had refused to partake in any assassination. And records do not indicate that whistles were found on Powell, Atzerodt, Herold, or any other person convicted at the trial. The rider was described as heading "northerly" past Massachusetts Avenue, which intersects 10th Avenue several blocks north of Ford's Theatre. But Booth was riding as rapidly as possible in the opposite direction, south, crossing the Navy Yard Bridge into Maryland.

One explanation that has been advanced: the whistles were used to send riders in diverse directions, in order to initially confuse police as to which way Booth had fled. Whether this explanation is correct or not, the use of multiple whistles does again imply that Booth was part of a wider conspiracy than the official story tells us.

The "New York Crowd"

In his long-lost confession, George Atzerodt also said:

> Booth said he had met a party in New York who would get the President certain. They were going to mine the end of the White House, next to War Dept. They knew an entrance to accomplish it through. Spoke about getting friends of the President to get up an entertainment; they would mix in it, have a serenade and thus get at the President and [his] party.
>
> These were understood to be projects.
>
> Booth said if he did not get him quick, the New York crowd would. Booth knew the New York party apparently by a sign. He [Atzerodt] saw Booth give some kind of sign to two parties on the avenue who he said were from New York.[26]

So Booth knew a group of New York entertainers who—allegedly—were planning to kill Lincoln through "friends of the President." These serenaders were also known as "minstrels." They typically performed in blackface.

Dan Bryant

Although Atzerodt didn't know their names, Booth, who often traveled to New York, had many actor friends in that community. This included:

- Minstrel Daniel Bryant, who gave Booth a diamond stickpin—the same stickpin Booth said he had a mind to give to Seward's chambermaid. This stickpin was mentioned by David Herold during his interrogation,[27] and was found on Booth's body at the Garrett farm, engraved "Dan Bryant to J. W. Booth."[28]

Like the diary and whistle, this stickpin wasn't presented in evidence at the trial; it simply vanished. At first I suspected theft—but being engraved to Booth, as stolen merchandise it would have had no resale value at a jeweler's at that time. Did it disappear because it connected the assassin to the New Yorkers instead of the Confederacy?

- Booth was well-known to carry a swagger stick (sometimes also described as a "cane," "riding crop," or even a "whip"). This item still exists and, as this book went to press, was being offered for $50,000 at the auction site *Uncrate* (https://uncrate.com/john-wilkes-booths-swagger-stick/). Screenshot on the following page.

The site says the stick's handle is gold-plated and engraved "Neal Bryant to J W Booth" (Neal, also spelled "Neil," was Dan Bryant's brother and a fellow minstrel). The site says Booth posed with it in 11 different photos.

This indicates not only that Booth was very close to the Bryants, but that the stick carried significance. It's doubtful that he repeatedly posed with it simply because he thought it attractive. It was more likely a means by which he could be identified as a member—perhaps a high-ranking member—of some organization, but only by people who were "initiated."

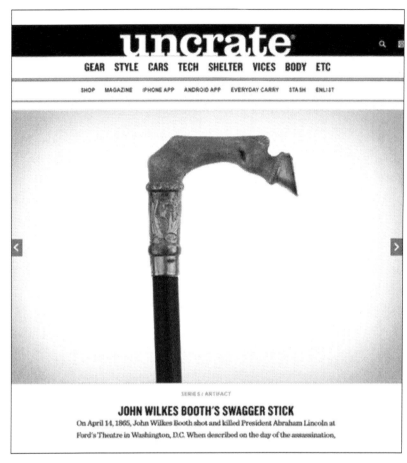

SERIES : ARTIFACT

JOHN WILKES BOOTH'S SWAGGER STICK

On April 14, 1865, John Wilkes Booth shot and killed President Abraham Lincoln at Ford's Theatre in Washington, D.C. When described on the day of the assassination,

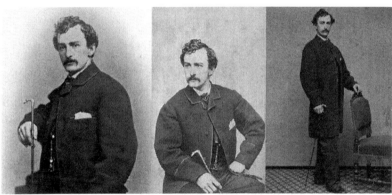

In his lost confession, Atzerodt said Booth knew the New Yorkers by "a sign." On January 18, 1869, the *Baltimore American and Advertiser* carried another confession, allegedly made by Atzerodt in his cell the night before his execution. He elaborated more on these secret signs, speaking of a woman in Booth's circle:

> Surratt was made known to her in New York by a signal conveyed by a small switch [stick] with a waxed end and a piece of red ribbon on the butt [handle], handled horizontally through the fingers. This sign was given on a hotel pavement on Broadway.[29]

Was Booth's swagger stick an emblem of a secret society?

▪ New York Actor Samuel Chester stated that Booth invited him to join his plot to kidnap Lincoln. Chester said he declined. Of the 366 witnesses called before the 1865 military tribunal, other than Louis Weichmann, only Chester admitted foreknowledge of the abduction scheme, but he wasn't punished for failing to report it. John T. Ford said:

> Some peculiar things transpired between Booth and myself, which made me wonder since that I was not more suspicious. He was exceedingly desirous at one time that I should engage an actor by the name of Samuel P. Chester, who was then engaged in performing minor parts at the Winter Garden [New York theater]. I told him I could not, in honor, take a man from a theatre where I thought he was bound to remain, and bring him to my theatre, although he would be a very desirable acquisition to my company.[30]

- William B. Donaldson had been, like the Bryants, a "New York minstrel." Immediately after the assassination, he fled Washington for Philadelphia, so quickly that he didn't bother packing his clothes.[31] He had been staying at the Simpson House, a saloon/hotel frequented by the minstrels that was only a block from Ford's Theatre. Post-assassination law enforcement reports said Donaldson was "a circus clown and Negro delineator," "is a well-known NY gambler and has been indicted as such." The reports described him as being engaged in suspicious activities and "that he might have some connection with the assassination of the late President."[32] He was arrested and put in Washington's Old Capitol Prison. But on the day the conspirators' trial began, the following message was sent:

> War Dept. Washington City, May 9th 1865
> Supt. W. S. Wood

Samuel Chester; William B. Donaldson

Old Capitol

Let the prisoner Wm. B. Donaldson be discharged.
By Order of the Secretary of War

H. L. Burnett
Brevet Co. and Judge Advocate[33]

No reason was given.

George Atzerodt said Booth identified members of the "New York Crowd" by a sign. Booth is widely believed to have been a member of the Knights of the Golden Circle, a pro-Southern secret society modeled after Freemasonry, with degrees and secret recognition signs. It is difficult to say with certainty whether Booth was a member, because secret societies normally keep their membership lists a tightly guarded secret. But given his Southern loyalty, and that the Knights were very active in the border state of Maryland, where the Booths long had their family home, it's probable that John was a member. Secret societies like to recruit prominent people.

Booth's kidnapping accomplice Michael O'Laughlen, a fellow Marylander, definitely admitted to police that he had joined the Knights four years earlier, though it is unclear if he remained a member.[34]

The Knights were infiltrated by Union agents. They had attempted to assassinate Lincoln in Baltimore in 1861, but were foiled thanks to being infiltrated by the Pinkerton Detective Agency—most famously by Kate Warne, America's first female detective, who could pose as a Southern belle with great skill. Her biography, easily found online, makes interesting reading.

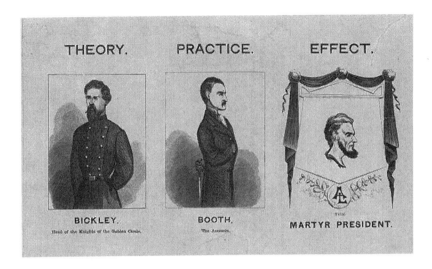

19th century depiction of Booth as a Knight of the Golden Circle. Charles Bickley was the founder of the Knights.

Having saved Lincoln's life once, why didn't the Pinkerton Detective Agency remain in Lincon's service? Because Pinkerton required strict honesty in order to maintain its reputation for integrity. Stanton didn't want that; he wanted a personal spy service, one he could use for his own purposes without regard for trifles such as truth or Constitutional rights. Thus the National Detective Bureau (later called the Secret Service) was established under Lafayette Baker; but when Stanton broke with Baker, he replaced him with William P. Wood.

We've seen that John Mathews' explanation of Booth's letter to the *Intelligencer* is riddled with doubts. He claimed that Booth, on horseback, spotted him on the street by happenstance and handed him the letter.

Given that Mathews evidently lied about the *Intelligencer* letter, it's probably reasonable to say Booth told Herold the truth about it—namely, that five other men signed it. This means that Booth would have attended a meeting on the 14th.

An eyewitness who contradicted Mathews' account was Louis Carland, who worked as a costumer at Ford's Theatre:

> The last time I saw Booth was on the day of the murder in front of the theater. He came up the street alone from E. Street, passed the time of day with me, stopped a few steps farther & Mr. Mathews was standing there. He took him by the arm and they walked up the street. That was the last I saw of him.[35]

Carland saw no horse, no envelope. Were Booth and Mathews headed for the Simpson House, the minstrels' hangout just one block away? Police heavily raided the Simpson House following the assassination, and there were many arrests; Lewis Mosby, the bartender, was arrested twice but released.[36] The explanation for police interest in the Simpson House is not recorded.

There is still another reason to believe Booth attended an April 14 meeting. Secretary of War Stanton and his assistant Major Eckert were evidently aware that the assassination was coming. That's why they lied to Abraham Lincoln in denying him the protection he wanted at Ford's Theatre. Mainstream historians claim the assassination plan existed only in Booth's mind that afternoon. How, then, did Stanton and Eckert know about it? ESP? Booth's convicted accomplices, Powell, Atzerodt and Herold, didn't learn there was a plan to murder until nearly 8PM. This suggests there was a gathering earlier in the day.

With his best kidnapping accomplices (John Surratt, Samuel Arnold, and Michael O'Laughlen) having abandoned him, Booth needed a new team. The most logical people for him to connect with were the "New York Crowd," whom he knew, and who already had an *alleged* plan to kill Lincoln. A likely place for the meeting would have been their hangout, the Simpson House.

This New York Crowd, whom Booth identified by a shared secret recognition sign, were very possibly members of the Knights of the Golden Circle, who had attempted to assassinate Lincoln in 1861.

People become more bold and violent when they're part of a mob than when alone. At the meeting, Booth was probably assured that *several* assassinations would occur that April 14. While Booth and Powell took out Lincoln and Seward, other assassins—the New Yorkers—would eliminate Grant and certain cabinet members, throwing the North into such disarray that the South might rally. Of course, there was no actual plot to kill any Radical Republican cabinet members. But the other so-called assassins, by cosigning Booth's letter, would convince him that he was not acting alone but as part of a big team. This could have been the moment Booth received inside information about Ford's Theatre, Lincon's bodyguard, and Seward's home, further emboldening him. This could be the moment Booth turned from kidnapper to assassin.

One of the cosigners, possibly Mathews, presumably took the letter and assured Booth that, the next day, he would deliver it to the *Intelligencer.*

Only he didn't. Instead, he delivered it straight to his "old friend" William P. Wood, who would have given it directly to his boss, Stanton. There, in ink, was Booth's commitment to kill the President. All systems were "go."

So when Booth later looked through the newspapers near Cox's farm, he not only realized the letter to the *Intelligencer* hadn't been published, but that no one else in the cabinet had been assassinated. He had been set up—double-crossed. This is probably what Booth meant when he wrote in what's left of his diary: "But its failure [the mission] was owing to others who did not strike for their country with a heart." Booth's diary was obviously intended, at least in part, to restate information lost in the *Intelligencer* letter, including accomplices' names. But the diary, like the letter, wound up in Stanton's hands, ensuring that would never happen.

Postscript: There's Something about John

John Wilkes Booth had a side that, to my knowledge, no historian has ever addressed. At first glance, it might appear to disagree with this book's narrative. But when broken down, I think it supports it, and is significant enough to discuss.

Sam Arnold, who had withdrawn from Booth's plot to kidnap Lincoln, wrote him a discreet letter on March 27, 1865, urging him to give up the idea. Excerpt:

> I told my parents I had ceased with you. Can I, then, under existing circumstances, come as you request? You know full well that the G—t [government] suspicions something is going on there; therefore, the undertaking is becoming more complicated. Why not, for the present, desist, for various reasons, which, if you look into, you can readily see, without my making any mention thereof.[37]

After the assassination, investigators found this letter inside a trunk in Booth's Washington hotel room. Booth had promised

Arnold he would destroy the letter, but he didn't.[38] Subsequently it became known as the "Sam letter" and was used at the conspiracy trial to convict Arnold.

In Arnold's memoirs, he wrote:

> Whether he left the letter in his trunk to betray me, in my innocence, into the hands of the government, through malice or forgetfulness, I cannot fathom.[39]

Arnold thought it possible that Booth tried to implicate him deliberately, but wasn't sure.

Then, in Atzerodt's room, police found a bankbook belonging to Booth, and a handkerchief belonging to Mary Booth (his mother). These items helped incriminate Atzerodt by concretely linking him to Booth. But Atzerodt wouldn't have possessed those things. Who might have planted them there? It could have been a detective, but might also have been Booth himself.

In his courtroom testimony about the abduction plot, Booth's friend Samuel Chester said:

> He urged the matter, and talked with me, I suppose, half an hour; but I still refused to give my assent. Then he said to me, "You will at least not betray me;" and added, "You dare not." He said he could implicate me in the affair anyhow.[40]

And in 1890, Mortimer Ruggles, one of the three Confederate soldiers who assisted Booth to the Garrett farm, recalled:

> That Andrew Johnson might appear to be implicated in the plot of assassination, Booth said that he had left that

morning a note at the hotel where the Vice-President lived, to compromise him.[41]

There's that word "implicate" again. Booth apparently considered that implicating others was one of his fortes. Mainstream historians claim that on the morning of April 14th, Booth suddenly became focused on planning to kill the President. Why, then, would he begin with an unessential detail like planting that card? Or was he—as actors professionally do—following a script that had already been given him? Of course, the card gave Stanton and his friends a tool of blackmail to keep Andrew Johnson in line, and they made use of it later during their attempt to impeach Johnson. Was it only coincidence that Stanton utilized Booth's subterfuge?

And what was Booth's most *conspicuous* act of implication? It occurred right at the assassination. In front of about 1,500 witnesses, he leaped onto the stage and reportedly shouted "Sic semper tyrannis" (Virginia's state motto) and "The South is avenged!" Thus he implicated the entire Confederacy in the assassination.

If Booth's only personal goal was to kill Lincoln, why choose such a challenging venue? The President was known to take walks, accompanied by just one bodyguard. Today we hear of drive-by shootings. Why didn't Booth attempt a "ride-by" shooting on the street? It would have been easier, and afforded a better opportunity for escape.

Some will argue that Booth's ego craved an audience. But the people at Ford's Theatre had their eyes glued to the stage. The only person who claimed to have actually witnessed Booth firing his shot was an audience member named James C. Ferguson.[42]

For Booth, the audience wasn't there to see the shooting, but to hear his proclamations about the South on stage. A plain street assassination could not have achieved such an outcome.

I must hasten to add that very legitimate objections can be raised to what I have just written. For Booth to implicate the South suggests that he was actually *anti-Southern*. Yet everything about Booth's life—his letters, his arguments with friends and family—show him to have been consistently pro-Southern.

I am aware, of course, that actors are capable of taking on false personas—they do that for a living. But for Booth to have assumed a fake pro-Southern persona, day in day out, for years, without ever showing his true hand, exceeds all bounds of credibility. Booth had supported the Confederacy since before the war's outbreak—years before he could have foreseen himself assassinating Lincoln.

Nonetheless, Booth's violence was directed at the only two ranking men in the administration—Lincoln and Seward—who sought reconciliation with the South. Why would Booth target them? Partly, perhaps, from ignorance about the conflict between Lincoln and his closest advisors; but mostly from false assurances from others at the meeting—the five cosigners of the *Intelligencer* letter—that they would assassinate the remainder of Lincoln's cabinet.

According to the official story, Booth met with Powell, Atzerodt and Herold on the evening of the 14th. The *only* cabinet member they tried assassinating was Seward. How would taking out that one man destabilize Lincoln's cabinet? Seward was bedridden from a serious carriage accident anyway—he wasn't even attending cabinet meetings. If Booth needed to plan killing

Lincoln, his primary objective, why even bother with Seward? From Booth's perspective, it only made sense if he believed other assassins were going to wipe out the rest of the cabinet. But from Stanton's perspective, it made complete sense, as it would eliminate the two prominent men who stood in the way of his plan for Reconstruction.

On April 14, Booth probably did meet with members of the Knights of the Golden Circle, or one of its offshoots. But just as occurred in the 1861 Lincoln assassination attempt, these were not true Knights; they were government infiltrators—"feds."

Secret societies usually demand strict obedience to orders. They also offer quid pro quo—do favors for them, and they'll do favors for you. What favors did Booth receive? A script for the assassination, inside information about Seward's home, promises that Lincoln's bodyguard would be missing, that the Presidential box would be prepped, that the telegraph wires would shut down, guaranteed safe passage out of Washington, and the illusion that he would receive a hero's welcome in the South, where, as he later told Herold, he was expecting to meet the other assassins. And what was Booth to give in return, besides shooting Lincoln? An agreement to plant the evidence against Johnson, and to shout from the stage that the South had been avenged. Booth may have been deceived into believing this pronouncement would vindicate the Confederacy. But to Stanton, it would *incriminate* the Confederacy, opening the door to brutal Reconstruction. In fact, Stanton probably couldn't have scripted the assassination much better than the way it happened.

Booth was allowed to escape, and, if not for his injury, might ultimately have made Mexico, or, by boat, another foreign country.

In his long-lost confession, George Atzerodt said, "Surratt bought a boat from Dick Smoot and James Brawner living about Port Tobacco, for which they paid $300.00."[43] The essence of this story was confirmed by Richard Smoot in his rare book published more than 40 years later, when Atzerodt's confession was still lost. Smoot wrote:

> I owned a good, large and stout boat … . I received a visit from John H. Surratt, who expressed a desire to purchase my boat … saying that it would be needed in an emergency which might arise within a very short amount of time. … I was inclined to associate the coming event with a plan to abduct Lincoln, concerning which plan I had heard vague rumors … . after some little time spent in negotiating with Surratt, I finally agreed to sell him the boat for two hundred and fifty dollars.[44]

According to Smoot, the boat was secreted on King's Creek, a branch of the Potomac. He believed that, after the assassination, Booth and any accomplices were heading for that boat, and to then "make their way to the seaboard, there board a vessel bound for some country with which the United States had no extradition treaty."[45]

Smoot believed Booth's downfall was his broken leg, which forced him to divert to Dr. Mudd's. The unforeseen injury seriously immobilized and delayed Booth, making his capture inevitable, and therefore necessitating both his murder and the concealment and defacing of his diary.

Notes

1. "John Surratt's 1870 Account of the Lincoln Assassination Conspiracy," (speech), *University of Missouri—Kansas City School of Law*, https://famous-trials.com/lincoln/2169-surrattspeech.

2. William C. Edwards and Edward Steers, eds., *The Lincoln Assassination: The Evidence* (Urbana: University of Illinois Press, 2009), Kindle edition, 682.

3. "Major Henry R. Rathbone: Testimony," *Historic Trial Transcripts*, https://tinyurl.com/4a2jhhyx.

4. *The Assassination of President Lincoln and the Trial of the Conspirators*, comp. Benn Pitman (New York: Moore, Wilstach & Baldwin, 1865), 82.

5. Ibid.

6. Don Thomas, *The Reason Lincoln Had to Die* (Chesterfield, Virginia: Pumphouse Publishers, 2013), 89.

7. Don Thomas, "The Cover-up of George Atzerodt's Confession," https://tinyurl.com/ymvft2bv.

8. "Margaret Coleman," *Seward Family Digital Archive*, https://sewardproject.org/person-public-fields/78313.

9. "Charles Sumner," *Wikipedia*, https://en.wikipedia.org/wiki/Charles_Sumner.

10. Edward Steers, *The Lincoln Assassination Encyclopedia* (New York: HarperCollins, 2010), Kindle edition, 95.

11. Edwards and Steers, 673.

12. *Impeachment Investigation* (Washington, D. C.: Government Printing Office, 1868), 674.

13. Edwards and Steers, 677.

14. Al Hunter, "John Mathews, Lincoln, Booth and Six Degrees of Separation," *The Weekly View*, February 25, 2016, https://tinyurl.com/2a6yutzv; "John Mathews on Booth Letter," *The New York Times*, July 19, 1867, https://tinyurl.com/4mwymvj3.

15. Don Thomas, *The Reason Booth Had to Die* (Chesterfield, Virginia: Pumphouse Publishers, 2017), 46; Edwards and Steers, 846-47.

16. Edwards and Steers, 1308.

17. Susan Wilson, "Boston, the Booth Brothers, and the Parker House," *BU School of Hospitality Administration*, May 11, 2015, https://tinyurl.com/3ktxvr99.

18. Thomas, *The Reason Lincoln Had to Die*, 53.

19. *Impeachment Investigation*, 533.

20. Ibid., 481.

21. Ibid., 492.

22. Ibid., 491.

23. *The Assassination of President Lincoln and the Trial of the Conspirators*, 95.

24. Edwards and Steers, 539.

25. Ibid., 138, 383, 534, 1042

26. Thomas, "The Cover-up of George Atzerodt's Confession."

27. Edwards and Steers, 682.

28. Ibid., 683.

29. Dave Taylor, "The Confessions of George Atzerodt," *LincolnConspirators*, August 30, 2020, https://tinyurl.com/5eajjdvx.

30. *Impeachment Investigation*, 534-35.

31. Edwards and Steers, 395.

32. Ibid., 916-17.

33. Ibid., 261.

34. Statement of Thomas Carmichael, Baltimore Marshal of Police; Edwards and Steers, 332.

35. Edwards and Steers, 330.

36. Ibid., 395.

37. "Letter from Samuel Arnold to John Wilkes Booth, March 27, 1865," *University of Missouri—Kansas City School of Law*, https://tinyurl.com/yza2erfz.

38. Samuel Bland Arnold, *Memoirs of a Lincoln Conspirator*, ed. Michael W. Kauffman (Westminster, Maryland: Heritage Books, 2008), 29.

39. Ibid., 50.

40. *The Assassination of President Lincoln and the Trial of the Conspirators*, 44.

41. Prentiss Ingraham, "Pursuit and Death of John Wilkes Booth," *The Century* (January 1890), 445.

42. Edwards and Steers, 489-90.

43. Taylor, "The Confessions of George Atzerodt."

44. Richard Mitchell Smoot, *The Unwritten History of the Assassination of Abraham Lincoln* (1908; reprint, London: Forgotten Books, 2012), 7-8.

45. Ibid., 19.

EPILOGUE

I n his book *The Reason Booth Had to Die*, Don Thomas wrote:

> The conspiracy to remove Lincoln from office consisted
> of four levels, with John Wilkes Booth and his New York
> accomplices at level 4. Secretary Stanton and his military
> subordinates were level 3. Congressional conspirators
> within Lincoln's own party, spearheaded by Charles
> Sumner, Thaddeus Stevens, and Salmon Chase were level 2.
> At level 1, were the Northeastern capitalists who used their
> deep pockets to buy Washington lobbyists, while providing
> financing to elect their chosen candidates for Congress.[1]

In other words, things were not much different than today.
Politicians were not the ultimate power; they simply represented
wealthy interests who remained in the background—what we now
label "the Deep State."

During Andrew Johnson's Presidency, tensions mounted
between him and Secretary of War Stanton, as Johnson became less
inclined toward the Radical Republican plan to subjugate the South.
He began moving toward leniency—Lincoln's postwar vision.

Then came "the straw that broke the camel's back." As
Eisenschiml notes, a revelation occurred during the 1867 trial of
John Surratt:

The junior counsel for the defense was addressing the jury at the trial of Mrs. Surratt's son in Washington. In the course of his speech he made a contemptuous reference to the petition for mercy which had been attached to the sentence of that unfortunate woman, now dead more than two years. The President, learning apparently from the papers that such a document existed, sent to the War Office for the findings of the court-martial. This was on August 5, 1867. Before nightfall he discharged Stanton by sending him a curt note:

> Sir:
>
> Public considerations of a high character constrain me to say that your resignation as Secretary of War will be accepted.
>
> ANDREW JOHNSON
> President of the United States.

The immediate consequence of Johnson's action was his [attempted] impeachment by Congress. This was what Stanton had been playing for. It was a game for big stakes. If Johnson should be found guilty, the War Minister would be the strongest man in the country; and the elections of 1868 were only a little over a year away. Destiny, however, willed it otherwise. One single senator stood between Stanton and the fulfillment of his dreams. By a vote of thirty-five to eighteen Johnson escaped impeachment. With the announcement of the result, Stanton collapsed. He relinquished his hold on the War Department where he had held forth for months behind barricades and an army of sentinels.[2]

Stanton was finally finished. On December 23, 1869, he was on his deathbed. He was visited by William P. Wood, who found the former War Secretary plagued by thoughts of Mary Surratt. Wood stated: "In his broken-down and depressed condition, he declared that he was haunted day and night by visions of the unfortunate woman, and that he could not live under the pressure he was bearing."[3]

The following day, Christmas Eve, Stanton died. Eisenschiml put it well:

> In view of the innumerable intrigues which dotted the life of Stanton and the countless death warrants he had signed without remorse, it is noteworthy that his last thoughts occurred with such disquietude on the comparatively unimportant conspiracy trial and its most prominent victim.[4]

There is one Judge no man can appoint, threaten, or bribe. Before he died, Samuel Arnold, last surviving member of the alleged assassination conspirators, also put it well:

> They have all passed to the bar of God, suffering on earth ended, silently awaiting justice at the hands of the Almighty, in whose presence truth shall be revealed. Man can hide it from his fellow-man, but the truth will be established before the bar of God.[5]

Historians, take note.

Notes

1. Don Thomas, *The Reason Booth Had to Die* (Chesterfield, Virginia: Pumphouse Publishers, 2017), v-vi.
2. Otto Eisenschiml, *Why Was Lincoln Murdered?* (1937; reprint, London: Sothis Press, 2023), 431-32.
3. Otto Eisenschiml, *In the Shadow of Lincoln's Death* (New York: Wilfred Funk, 1940), 187.
4. Ibid., 188.
5. Samuel Bland Arnold, *Memoirs of a Lincoln Conspirator*, ed. Michael W. Kauffman (Westminster, Maryland: Heritage Books, 2008), 59-60.

INDEX

abduction plot, 9, 64-65, 79-80, 86-87, 97, 109-110
Arnold, Robert, 91-92
Arnold, Samuel, 9, 59-60, 64, 71, 79-80, 81, 83, 104, 110, 133, 135-36, 147
Atzerodt, George, 8, 9, 30-33, 64, 75, 82-83, 85, 92, 99, 110, 114-16, 119, 125, 126, 127, 129, 131, 133, 136, 138, 140
Augur, Christopher, 86

Bainbridge, Absalom, 51, 54
Baker, Lafayette, 44, 62, 63, 132
Baker, Luther, 44-48, 57, 99
Barnes, Joseph K., 53, 55
Basehart, Richard, 107
Bates, David Homer, 13, 14, 15
Bingham, John, 118
Booth, Asia, 54
Booth, Edwin, 78
Booth, John Wilkes, *passim*
  abduction plot of. *See* abduction plot
  Andrew Johnson, card left for by, 32-33, 136-37
  autopsy of, 53-56
  confidence in his assassination plan, 20-22
  conspiracy larger than assumed and, 109-40
  controversy over whether he lived on, 51-57
  death of, 8, 48, 53
  diary of, 61-70, 76, 102-103, 124, 135
  implication of others by, 135-38

  inside information provided to, 111-18
  Intelligencer letter and, 118-24, 132-33, 134-35, 138
  South's reaction to, 25
  target choices of, 22-27
  swagger stick of, 127-29
  whistle of, 124-25
Booth, Mary, 31, 75-76, 136
Boyd, James William, 53
Brawner, James, 140
Brophy, John P., 89
Bryant, Dan, 52-53, 126-27
Bryant, Neil, 127
Bryant, William L., 51
Burnett, H. L., 70, 88, 131
Burroughs, Joseph, 18
Butler, Benjamin, 64-65, 66, 68

Carland, Louis, 133
Chase, Salmon, 145
Chester, Samuel, 129, 130, 136
civil liberties, 23, 59, 91
Cobb, Silas, 117-18
Coleman, Margaret, 116-17
Conger, Everton, 44-48, 57, 63
conspiracy trial, 46, 59-72, 75-93
  conditions of prisoners during, 18-19, 59-61, 103-104
  hanging, 8-9, 89-93
  perjury at, 70-71, 80, 87-88, 93
Corbett, Boston, 8, 45, 48-49, 98, 103
Cox, Samuel, 41, 51, 78, 119
Coyle, John F., 119

Cristy, David, 25
Crook, William, 12-13, 15, 16

Davis, Jefferson, 25, 70-72, 87, 105
Dawson, Charles, 54
Dawson, Sarah Morgan, 25
DeWitt, David M., 65
diary of John Wilkes Booth, 61-70, 76
    FBI analysis of, 66-70, 103
Doherty, Edward, 44
Donaldson, James, 115-16, 117
Donaldson, William B., 130-31
Doster, W. E., 114
Dry Tortugas, 77, 78, 80-81, 99, 103-104

Eckert, Thomas, 13-14, 15, 35-38, 63,
    111, 118, 133
Edwards, William C., 48, 100
Eisenschiml, Otto, 1-2, 11, 12, 14, 25, 29,
    31, 32, 33, 36, 38, 39, 51, 61, 71, 85,
    89, 100-104, 107, 108, 145, 147
evidence, nature of, 105-106

FBI analysis of Booth diary, 66-70, 103
Ferguson, James C., 137
Fisher, George P., 94
Ford, Henry, 54
Ford, John T., 54, 122, 129
Fort Jefferson, 78, 80-81
Foster, John A., 124

Gardner, Alexander, 92
Garrett, R. B., 45
Garrett, Richard, 8, 43
Gleason, Daniel H. L., 85-87, 97
Grant, Julia, 6, 11-12, 30
Grant, Ulysses S., 5, 6, 7

alleged assassination attempt on, 30
invitation to Ford's Theatre declined by,
    11-12

Habeas Corpus Suspension Act, 23
Hall, James, 121
Hall, James O. (historian), 101, 103
Hamilton, H. L., 81
Hanchett, William, 101-105, 108
Hancock, W. S., 91
Hardie, James, 91
Harris, Clara, 6, 112
Harris, Ira, 6
Harris, Kamala, 3
Herold, David, 6, 7, 8, 9, 31, 41, 43, 45,
    51, 52, 69, 77, 78, 83, 92, 98, 99, 112,
    117-19, 120, 127, 132, 133, 138
Higgins, Clay, 3
Hitchcock, Alfred, 105
Holt, Joseph, 46-48, 61, 63, 64, 89, 102
House Judiciary Committee, 15, 36,
    45-46, 62, 63, 70, 122-23
Hughes, John J., 51

impeachment trial of Andrew Johnson,
    33, 146-47
Intelligencer, 7
    Booth's letter to, 118-24, 132-33,
    134-35, 138

January 6 "Insurrection," 2-3
Jett, Willie, 51, 52
Johnson, Andrew, 19-20, 35, 54, 78, 81,
    89-90, 145
    alleged assassination attempt on, 7, 8,
    30-33, 75, 83, 114
    card left by Booth for, 32-33, 136-37

impeachment attempt, 33, 122, 137,
    146-47
Jones, Thomas, 41, 51, 78, 119
Julian, George, 24

kidnapping plot. *See* abduction plot
King, Preston, 90
Knights of the Golden Circle, 131-32,
    134, 139

Lane, James Henry, 90
Lee, Robert E., 5, 11, 25, 107
Lincoln, Abraham, *passim*
    abduction plot and. *See* abduction plot
    assassination foreseen by, 12-13, 15
    death of, 6, 7
    deserted by bodyguard, 16-17, 111
    postwar plans for South of, 22-26
    South's response to death of, 25
    Stanton's denial of protection to, 13-15
Lincoln, Mary Todd, 5-6, 11-12, 17
Lundberg, Ferdinand, 106

Mathews, John, 119-24, 132-33, 134
May, John Frederick, 54, 55-56
McDevitt, James, 86
McPhail, James, 114
Merrill, William, 54
Merritt, James B., 70
Mosby, Lewis, 133
Mudd, Samuel, 7, 9, 41, 51, 52, 64, 76-79,
    80, 81, 104, 140
Murphy, Edward V., 87-88

National Detective Bureau, 44, 132
    See also Secret Service
"New York Crowd," 126-34

O'Beirne, James, 43-44, 87
O'Laughlen, Michael, 9, 79, 80, 81, 110,
    131, 133
Old Capitol Prison, 121-24, 130
Olin, Abram, 112-13

Parker, John F., 16-17, 20, 21, 103,
    111-12
Payne, Lewis. *See* Powell, Lewis
Peddicord, John, 54
Pinkerton Detective Agency, 131-32
Powell, Lewis, 7, 8, 9, 30-31, 64, 75, 82,
    90, 92, 110, 113-14, 115, 118, 125,
    133, 134, 138
Pumphrey, John, 18

Queensbury, Elizabeth, 51

Radical Republicans, 22-27, 33, 71, 109,
    117, 145
Rath, Christian, 92
Rathbone, Henry, 6, 14, 17, 21, 112
Raymond, Julian E., 48
Reconstruction, 22-26, 109, 139
Rickards, William, 62-63
reward money for helping capture
    assassination suspects, 41-42, 47-48,
    57, 80, 94
Robinson, George, 7, 115
Rogers, A. J., 61
Ruggles, Mortimer, 33, 51, 136

"Sam letter," 135-36
Secret Service, 44, 62
    See also National Detective Bureau
Seward, Fanny, 116
Seward, Frederick, 7

Seward, William, 7, 25-26, 30, 75, 82, 99,
    113-16, 125, 134, 138-39
Sharp, Joshua W., 86
Simpson House, 130, 133, 134
Slater, Sarah, 85
Smith, John L., 114
Smoot, Richard, 140
Spalding, Archbishop Martin John, 91
Spangler, Edman "Ned," 18-20, 59, 80,
    81, 104
Stanton, Edwin, *passim*
    alleged assassination attempt on, 29-30
    amnesia concerning Lincoln's April 14
        visit, 15-16
    assassination investigation takeover by,
        7, 35
    behavior immediately after
        assassination, 35-39
    Booth's diary and, 61-64, 69-70
    canvas head bags for prisoners
        invented by, 18-19, 59-60
    deathbed thoughts of, 147
    delay in reporting Booth as assassin, 38
    denial of protection sought by
        Lincoln, 12-15
    dismissal of charges against
        Corbett by, 49
    Dry Tortugas prisoners and, 80-81
    failure to close Booth's escape road, 39
    Grant warned by, 12
    Jefferson Davis, attempt to
        incriminate, 70-72
    Mary Suratt's final sacraments and,
        90-91
    select detachment sent after Booth by,
        43-44
    summary of evidence against, 97-99
    split with Andrew Johnson, 145-47

withdrawal of John Surratt reward by, 93
Steers, Edward, 101-102, 105-108
Stevens, Thaddeus, 71, 145
Stewart, James, 105
Stuart, Richard, 51, 69
Sumner, Charles, 117, 145
Surratt, Anna, 90
Surratt, John, 9, 41, 83-85, 87, 93-94, 99,
    110, 129, 133, 140
    trial of, 94, 146
Surratt, Mary, 8, 19, 59, 65, 83-84, 87-93,
    99, 146, 147

Tanner, James, 38
Taylor, Walker, 71
telegraph system, 35
    disruption of after assassination, 36-38
They've Killed President Lincoln
    (TV documentary), 107
Thomas, Don, 2, 48, 51, 53, 66, 69, 70,
    90, 108, 121, 145
Todd, George Brainard, 53
Townsend, George A., 37
trial. *See* conspiracy trial; impeachment
    trial of Andrew Johnson; Suratt,
    John, trial of,
Trindal, Elizabeth, 93

Verdi, Tullao, 114

Walker, R. W., 121
Wallace, Lew, 77
Walter, Jacob, 90-91
War Department, 12-16, 23, 35, 43,
    84-88, 90-91, 94, 99, 109, 114
Warne, Kate, 131
Wiechmann, Louis, 84-89, 109, 129
Winkler, H. Donald, 62-63

Wood, William P., 121-24, 130, 132, 134, 147

Woodward, Joseph Janvier, 53

Printed in Great Britain
by Amazon

54655668R00088